RELAY

STUDENT'S BOOK

2

LUCY HALE

Arnold/Topaz

Edward Arnold

A division of Hodder & Stoughton

LONDON   MELBOURNE   AUCKLAND

Illustrated by Dave Farris, David LaGrange, Jenny Mumford, Julia Osorno, Sue Smith, Rodney Sutton.

Thanks are due to the following copyright owners for permission to reproduce their photographs:

Allsport: pp 13r (Gary Mortimore), 77tr, lr, rc;
Associated Press: p 73;
Barnaby's Picture Library: pp 38r, 72r:
The Bridgeman Art Library: p 72l;
Robert Harding Picture Library: pp 17t, b, 26, 36l, bl.57t;
Daisy Hayes: pp 5, 10, 25, 29, 36, l, 45, 51;
Kodak Ltd: p 25t;
Steve Richards: pp 25b, 27(all), 36c, 38l (all), 56 (all):
Rex Features Ltd: pp 31, 57b, 72b, 74, 77rb;
Bob Thomas Picture Library: pp 131, c, 77lb;
Toppix's Press, Liverpool; 17c.

© 1990 Topaz Projects Limited

First published in Great Britain 1990

Designed by Janet McCallum

British Library Cataloguing in Publication Data

Hale, Lucy
  Relay two.
  I. Title
  428

  ISBN 0–340–51681–X

Typeset in 11/12pt Palatino by TecSet Ltd, Wallington, Surrey. Printed and bound in Great Britain for Edward Arnold, the educational, academic and medical publishing division of Hodder and Stoughton Limited, Mill Road, Dunton Green, Sevenoaks, Kent TN13 2YA by Cambus Litho, East Kilbride.

Contents

It's the first day at Southford College. Janet, a new student, is sad because she doesn't know anybody. Mike is an old student. Read the cartoon strip.

INTRODUCE YOURSELF TO OTHER STUDENTS IN THE CLASSROOM.

2 Write and act out a similar dialogue with another student.

WOULD YOU LIKE A DRINK OF WATER?

YES, PLEASE.

1 Frank and Teresa are students at a language school in England. They are at a party. Read the dialogue between Frank and Teresa and put the lines in order.

A Hello, Frank. I'm Teresa.
B Where are you from, Teresa?
C Hello, I'm Frank. What's your name?
D Would you like to dance?
E No, thanks. I'm on a diet.
F I'm from Colombia. And you?
G I'd love to.
H Would you like a piece of cake?
I I'm from Germany.

Episode 1

Sam and Lucy were spring cleaning the house for their mother. They were on holiday and their mother was at work. They wanted to surprise her when she got back.

Sam was cleaning the loft when he found a dusty box. It was the size of a shoe box. He opened it. Inside the box there was a packet of letters with old stamps on them. His heart beat fast. He shouted 'Lucy!' and told her to take a break because he had something to show her.

Lucy looked angry when she walked up to the loft. 'I was cleaning the windows downstairs,' she said. 'I'm sorry,' said Sam, 'but look what I found.' He showed her the letters. She took one and took the letter out of its envelope. The first thing she saw was "Dear Mary,". 'That's Mum's name!' she cried. 'I wonder who wrote these letters.'

Sam took another letter. 'Yes, this is to Mum too.' He quickly looked for the name of the sender. It simply said: "Best wishes, D.". 'I wonder who this D. is,' said Sam. 'Perhaps it's one of Mum's old boyfriends,' laughed Lucy. 'Let's have a look at the address of the sender,' said Sam. It was in Liverpool.

True or false?
1 Sam and Lucy were on holiday.
2 They are cousins.
3 Their mother has got a job.
4 Sam found some photographs in a box.
5 The letters had old stamps on them.
6 Lucy was busy when Sam called her.
7 The letters were to their mother.
8 The sender's name was Charles.
9 Sam found the letter in the kitchen.
10 The sender lived in Liverpool.

WHAT DO YOU THINK WILL HAPPEN NEXT?

1 Complete this table:

He	was		England.	He is English.
She			Canada.	She
I			Japan.	I
We			Spain.	We are Spanish.
They			Italy.	They
You	were		China.	You
He		born in	Denmark.	He
She	was		Holland.	
I			Turkey.	
We			Portugal.	
They			France.	
You			Greece.	

2 Find the nationalities from the table above in this square below:

A	Z	H	I	X	F	R	E	N	C	H	T
D	U	T	C	H	S	V	G	T	D	N	A
I	Y	O	A	H	P	W	U	C	A	P	F
Z	N	C	I	T	A	L	I	A	N	O	K
B	G	A	Y	J	N	X	C	E	I	R	S
N	E	N	G	L	I	S	H	M	S	T	V
U	D	A	E	D	S	W	I	L	H	U	J
C	F	D	M	A	H	B	N	Q	L	G	P
G	X	I	H	G	R	E	E	K	O	U	R
D	J	A	P	A	N	E	S	E	B	E	F
I	K	N	J	C	B	O	E	K	P	S	P
M	R	L	T	U	R	K	I	S	H	E	S

1 Before you listen to the telephone conversation, answer these questions:
1 What do you call a doctor for animals?
2 Imagine that you answer the phone and someone wants to speak to your friend but your friend is out. What do you say?

2 Listen to the telephone conversation and fill in the gaps.

3 Now work in pairs. Student A looks at page 92 – A Telephone Message – and Student B looks at page 93 – A Telephone Message.

> Janet,
>   Your friend _____ phoned. He _____ meet you ____ 3 o'clock _____ because his _____ is _____ and he has to _____ him to the vet. Can you _____ him when you get home?
>
>   Mum

A Survey

Activities

1 What questions do you usually ask people when you meet them?

2 What would you like to know about the other people in the group?

3 Write out a list of 10 questions to find out about the things you mentioned in 2.
E.g.: 1 What's your name?
    2 Where are you from?
    3 What is your favourite animal?
    4

4 Draw a chart to write any useful information about the group.

name	nationality	favourite animal	

5 Use your questions to interview every person in the group and write their answers in your chart.

6 Do you have anything in common with the other people in your group?

2 After the Concert

I Cilla, Julia and Janet are friends. They are going home after a Michael Jackson concert.

I'd like a suit like Michael Jackson's.

So would I!

I wouldn't. I don't like his clothes, but I think he's a great singer.

Cilla   Janet   Julia

1 *Cilla:* Yes, so do I, but I also like his clothes.
Janet: I really enjoyed his concert.
Julia: I didn't. It was too crowded. I'm very tired now.
5 *Cilla:* I'm not.
Janet: Neither am I.
Julia: Let's have a hamburger or something. I'm very hungry.
Janet: Are you? I'm not.
10 *Cilla:* Neither am I.
Julia: Well, I need to eat something. I'm going into the next hamburger place. You can come with me or you can go home.
Cilla: Don't be silly! Of course we're coming
15 with you.

. . . .
(half an hour later)
. . . .

Julia: Ah! I enjoyed that hamburger.
20 *Cilla:* So did I. I think I was hungry.
Janet: I wasn't and now I've got stomach ache.

Answer these questions:
1 Why does Janet say 'So would I.' in the picture?
2 Why does Julia say 'I didn't.' in line 3?
3 Why does Janet say 'Neither am I.' in line 6?
4 Do you like Michael Jackson? Why?/Why not?

I can't sing!

Neither can I!

2 Agree or disagree:
a I can't speak Chinese.
b I love dancing.
c I can swim.
d I'm not English.
e She's speaking English.

I've got a lot of money.

I haven't.

3 Talk about these topics with a friend:
a punks   **b** school
c dentists   **d** pets
E.g.:
A – I think punks are silly.
B – Do you? I don't. I think they are interesting.
or – So do I.

KEEP OFF THE GRASS

Who doesn't know Tommy? He's everybody's favourite pop-star. Well, we interviewed him about his hobby. This guy is crazy!

Some people collect stamps, some people build model planes, there are many hobbies, but Tommy's hobby is really unusual: he collects . . . SUNGLASSES!!!

He's got 375 pairs of sunglasses. He buys them when he travels abroad. His favourite pair of sunglasses is the pair he bought in Japan last year.

He wears a different pair of sunglasses every day!

1 Answer these questions:
a What hobbies are mentioned in the passage?
b Can you think of other hobbies?
c Have you got a hobby?

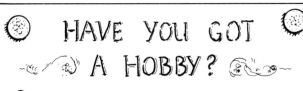

HAVE YOU GOT A HOBBY?

Do you know other people who have the same hobby you have?

COME AND MEET THEM AT:

The Hobby Centre,
28, Maple Rd.,
London W 12.

2 Where would you find a notice like this one?

3 Answer these questions:
a What is the difference between a hobby and a sport?
b Do you practise any sport?

4 Write a notice similar to the one on the left inviting people to come to a sports centre.

5 Interview other people in the group and find out about their hobbies and about the sport they practise.

Episode 2

Sam and Lucy found a box with old letters for their mother in the loft. The letters are signed 'D.' and D.'s address is in Liverpool.

What was your answer to the last question of episode 1? (see page 5.)

Listen to episode 2 and then answer these questions:

1 Why did Sam want to go to Liverpool?
2 Was Liverpool near the place where they lived?
3 How much money did Lucy have?
4 How much money did Sam have?
5 How much did a coach ticket to Liverpool cost?
6 What did Lucy want to do?
7 Where did the coach leave from?
8 What was Sam's idea?
9 What did Lucy think of Sam's idea?
10 Do you think that Sam's idea was a good one?

Do you know the names of all these animals?
Write their names in the grid below and find out
the name of a very popular British hobby.

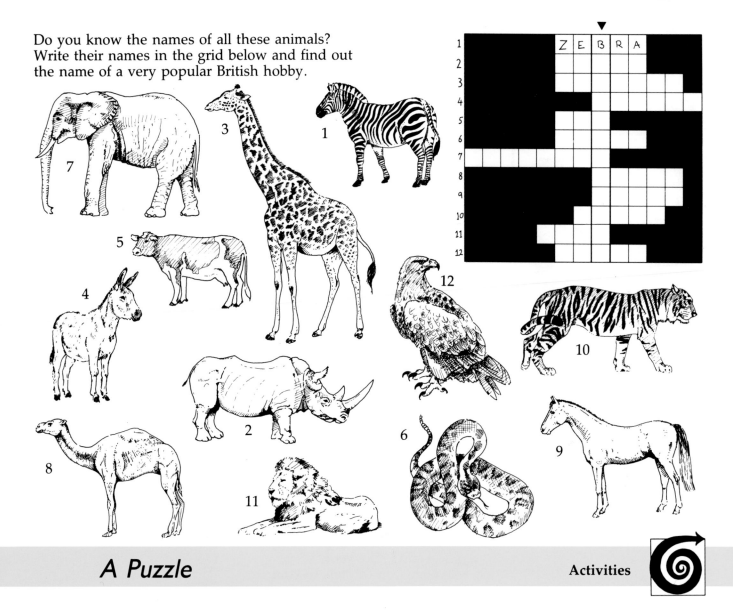

A Puzzle

Activities

1 Mark, John, Sara and Jean are friends. Mark's a boy and so is John. Sara isn't a boy and neither is Jean.

2 They all like different sweets and they practise different sports.

3 Mark plays a team game but he doesn't like toffee.

4 The girl who likes mints also likes swimming.

5 John doesn't like gymnastics or chocolate.

6 Jean likes wine gums.

people: Mark John Sara Jean
sweets: mints wine gums toffee chocolate
sports: gymnastics tennis football swimming

Find out who likes what and who practises what. Complete the chart below:

name	sweet	sport

1 Read the article and answer these questions:

1 Can you go on your own?
2 Can you play loud music on the coach?
3 Can you get on the coach without a packed lunch?
4 Can you take a camera with you?

Nobody likes to wait or worry, so remember:
You must be there on time.
You must stay with the group.

You are travelling with other people, so remember:
You mustn't play loud music on the coach.

The driver has to concentrate, so remember:
You mustn't talk to the driver when he is driving.

You may be away all day, so remember:
You need to take a packed lunch.

You will walk a lot, so remember:
You need to wear comfortable shoes.

You haven't got a camera? Don't worry!
You needn't take a camera because you can buy postcards.
You needn't take your walkman: you can talk to your friends for a change!

2 At School:

There are some things we must do at school, there are some things we mustn't do, there are some things we need to do and there are some things we needn't do.

In pairs, ask and answer questions like this:

A Do we have to wear a uniform?
B Yes, we must wear a uniform. or: No, we needn't wear a uniform.
A Can we chew gum in class?
B No, we mustn't chew gum in class.

Use these words:
1 have to/wear/uniform
2 have to/buy present/teacher
3 can/speak/Italian
　　　　　　Spanish
　　　　　　etc.
4 have to/bring/pen
5 have to/wear/hat

6 can/fall/asleep
7 have to/English
8 have to/clean/classroom
9 have to/do/homework
10 have to/listen/teacher
11 can/drink/in class
12 have to/bring/paper

1 Answer these questions and then discuss your answers with a partner:

a What are the Olympic Games?

b How often can we see them?

c Do you watch the Olympic Games on T.V.?

d Would you like to be an athlete? Why?/Why not?

2 Read the first part of a magazine article about an athlete's life:

Every four years we watch the Olympic Games on T.V. We see hundreds of men and women competing. The pictures are exciting. We see the winners smiling. We also see the spectators clapping and cheering.

But the life of an athlete is not easy. To take part in the games, they must train hard every day. For this they need loose clothes and comfortable shoes because tight clothes restrict their movements and uncomfortable shoes can hurt their feet.

3 Now, in groups, read the rest of the article and work together to write four lists:

athletes			
must	mustn't	need (to)	needn't
train hard every day		loose clothes comfortable shoes	

There is a programme for young people on the radio. On this programme, there is a section called 'Star Advice'. In this section, people write in to ask for advice and famous stars give them advice.

1 Today, Tommy, a famous pop star, is giving advice. Listen to him and fill in the chart below:

name	problem	advice			
		must	mustn't	need	needn't

2 Now you give some advice to these people:

> *Dear Star,*
> *I'm very sad. The other day I went to visit my best friend as usual, but her mother told me that she didn't want to speak to me. After that, I met her in the street, but she didn't say hello to me.*
> *What can I do?*
> *Sara*

> *Dear Star,*
> *My brother hates me because I'm going out with his best friend. I don't want to upset my brother, but I don't want to stop seeing his friend.*
> *Jill*

> *Dear Star,*
> *I hate my younger sister. She is going out with my best friend and now he doesn't want to come with me to the football on Saturdays.*
> *I want my best friend back.*
> *Mark*

> *Dear Star,*
> *I want to stop studying and get a job. I want to earn money. Is this a good idea?*
> *Harry*

All these pictures are related to travel. The words that correspond
to the pictures are listed below, but the letters are not in order.
Can you re-order them?

1 spotdrac = ...

2 pogur readel = ...

3 kadecp chunl = ...

4 uxinercos = ...

5 ritan = ...

6 orelapnae = ...

7 arcaem = ...

8 lothe = ...

9 mesumu = ...

10 hacco = ...

Where am I? – Game   Activities

Think of a place . . . (E.g.: a swimming pool).
Don't tell anybody what place you are thinking
of!
The other students have to guess what place you
are thinking of by asking you questions. You can
only answer 'yes' or 'no'.
E.g.: Can we sleep in this place?
       Must we wear a uniform in this place?
       Do we need to wear a uniform in this
       place?
       Can we swim in this place?
Take turns to think of places and to ask
questions.

4 A Helpful Friend

1 Read the cartoon strip and find:
a two ways of offering help
b a way of saying 'no' to **a**
c a way of saying 'yes' to **a**
d a way of asking for help
e a way of saying 'yes' to **d**

2 Can you think of ways of saying 'no' when someone asks for help?

The students at Southford College organize a disco evening every month. They take turns to clean the hall after each disco. It's Mike and Janet's turn this time.

JOE IS A FRIEND OF MIKE'S.

Hi. Can I give you a hand?

Yes please!

DISCO

TONIGHT

BUT JOE IS CLUMSY AND BREAKS A FEW THINGS.

EXIT

Oh no!

THE NEXT DAY...

Shall I clean the seats for you?

No thanks. We can do it ourselves.

JANET IS DOING THE SHOPPING FOR HER MOTHER.

These bags are very heavy... Joe is sad, he wants to help.

Nobody needs me... ≡SNIFF≡

JANET HAS A BRIGHT IDEA.

Could you carry these for me? They're very heavy.

Certainly.

3 What do you say in these situations?
1 You are going on holiday and you ask your friend to feed your canary.
2 A friend offers to take your dog for a walk but you enjoy doing that yourself.
3 A friend asks you to do his homework for him. You think that this is wrong.
4 The doorbell is ringing and you're very busy. Ask your friend to open the door.
5 Your friend asks you to buy a postcard for her. You want to help her.
6 Your friend looks worried. You want to help him.

Episode 3

Sam and Lucy decide to investigate who wrote the letters they found.

It was cold when Sam and Lucy caught the coach early in the morning.

'I'm glad I brought my coat,' said Lucy.

The coach moved through the heavy London traffic towards the motorway. Later that morning, as the bus raced past fields, it began to get warmer.

After about an hour, Sam shouted, 'Hey, look at those sheep!' 'Yes,' said Lucy, 'and look at those cows!' Sam and Lucy lived in a city and they didn't usually see sheep or cows.

About an hour later, they saw a sign indicating that Liverpool was six miles away.

'I thought it took longer to get to Liverpool,' said Lucy.

The coach drove into the city. Sam and Lucy thought that it looked very dirty. 'It isn't very nice,' said Lucy. 'I'm sure that there are nice parts,' Sam answered. 'Maybe the address we're looking for is in a nice part.' Lucy immediately felt better.

When the coach entered the station, Sam and Lucy got off. Sam saw a man in uniform. He went up to the man to ask him where the address was. 'You want to go to the Pier Head, son,' the man said. 'You can catch a bus at the Pier Head for West Derby. That's where the address is,' and then he told them how to get to the Pier Head.

Sam and Lucy saw many things. Here are some of them. Put them in the order Sam and Lucy saw them:
a part of the city of Liverpool
b fields
c a man in uniform
d heavy traffic
e Liverpool coach station
f the coach
g some animals in the fields
h a sign indicating that Liverpool was six miles away

Margaret is a 15-year-old girl. Her mother left her this note:

> Margaret,
>   I have to go to Gran's. I haven't got time to water the plants. Could you do it for me? and, could you take Fido for a walk, please?
>   Thanks
>   Mum
>   ——
>
>   P.S. Your room is very untidy and your shoes are very dirty. You must tidy your room and polish your shoes today.

1 Jill is Margaret's friend. She wants to go to the park because it's a lovely day. She is talking to Margaret now. Here is the dialogue, but it is not in order. Can you re-order it?

A Margaret: Could you? Oh, thanks!
B Jill: Shall I polish your shoes?
C Jill: Don't worry. I can help you.
D Jill: Let's see . . . Oh, dear!
E Margaret: Yes, please. I'll clean my room.
F Margaret: I can't. I've got lots to do. Look! Mum left this note.
G Margaret: And I've got to do my homework.
H Jill: It's a lovely day today. Let's go for a walk in the park.

. . . . . .

(some minutes later)

. . . . . .

A Jill: Certainly!
B Jill: Finished!
C Margaret: Thank you. Now, could you water the plants, please?

. . . . . .

(after a while)

A Jill: O.K. But hurry up.
B Jill: Shall I take your dog for a walk now?
C Jill: Do your homework?!?! Sorry, I can't.
D Margaret: No, we can do that together. Could you do my homework, please?
E Margaret: I'm only joking! Here, read this magazine while I do my homework.

2 Listen to the dialogue and check your answer.

There is a saying in English related to work and cooperation, people working together and helping other people. You can find this saying in the grid below. Just write the names of the parts of the house, numbered in the picture.

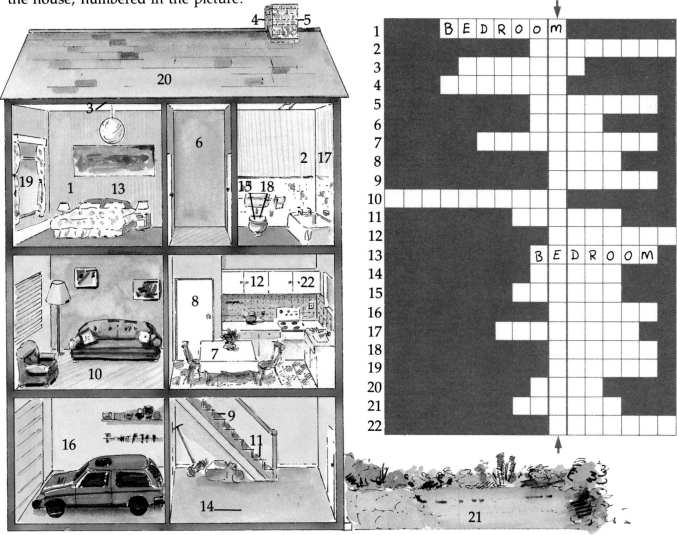

The Yes/No Game **Activities**

We use the words 'yes' and 'no' very often. Can you think of other ways of saying 'yes' and 'no'? E.g.: **A** Do you like chocolate?
B I certainly do.
A Are you English?
B I'm not.

1 Write two lists of expressions, one for 'yes' and one for 'no'.

2 Now use those expressions to play the yes/no game: One student sits at the front of the class and the other students ask him/her questions. The student at the front mustn't say 'yes' or 'no'. If the person at the front can last 1 minute without saying 'yes' or 'no', he/she wins.

Do you remember Janet? She's from Canada.

Janet: . . . but I don't know what to do. My father is a businessman and he wants me to study Economics but I don't like Economics. I don't know what to do!

Paul: There's a careers adviser at the college. He'll help you.

Janet: That's a great idea! I'll go and see him tomorrow.

Paul: Good luck!

. . . . . .

(at the advisers)

. . . . . .

Janet: Can you help me? I have to choose a career but I can't make up my mind. My father wants me to study Economics.

Adviser: And, do you like Economics?

Janet: Not really.

Adviser: What are you studying now at college?

Janet: I'm studying literature and French.

Adviser: So you like languages?

Janet: I really like literature. I'd like to read French novels in French.

Adviser: You can study French literature at university.

Janet: Will I have to sit any exams to enter university?

Adviser: No, but you'll need good marks at college.

Janet: I'll study very hard.

Adviser: I'm sure you will.

Janet: And I'm going to tell my father that I want to study literature.

Adviser: Will he understand?

Janet: I don't know.

I Answer these questions:

1 Paul says 'He'll help you'. Who's 'he'?

   What does Janet decide to do when Paul tells her about the careers adviser?

3 What will Janet need to enter university?

4 What does Janet promise to do to get good marks?

5 What does Janet decide in the end?

6 Do you think that her father will understand?

A surgery is the place where doctors see their patients. It could be in a hospital or in a house.
This is a picture of a noticeboard at a doctor's surgery.

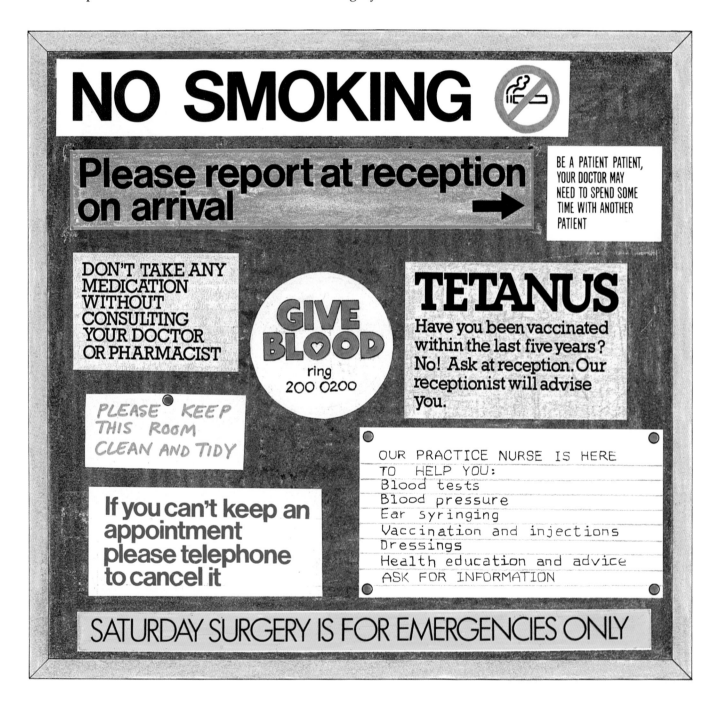

1 Read the notices and find four different jobs mentioned.

2 Now write a list of things each one of these jobs involves.

Across:
1 This person catches thieves.
8 This person teaches you English.
10 This person is the boss on a ship.
12 This person works with machines or engines.
13 This person checks your teeth.
15 This person works in a theatre.
16 This person writes books.
17 This person works in a circus.
18 This person sells meat.
19 This person repairs cars.

Down:
2 This person plays a musical instrument.
3 This person looks after patients in a hospital.
4 This person treats patients.
5 This person sings songs.
6 This person works in an office.
7 This person designs houses.
9 This person studies science.
11 This person paints pictures (or walls).

14 This person works on board a ship.
18 This person sells bread.

Can you think of other jobs or professions?

Look at the professions,
● which is the most difficult?
● which is the easiest?
● which is the most dangerous?

Future Plans

❙ A journalist interviewed some students at a secondary school. Listen to the interviews and fill in the chart below:

name	age	parents' occupation	what she wants to be

2 Write a short paragraph about your plans for the future.

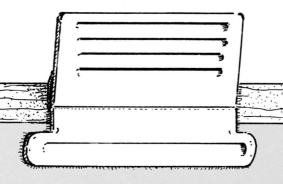

I What is a survey?
You are going to find out about other people's plans for the future.
To do this, you have to write a questionnaire.
You also need a sheet of paper to write the answers people give you.
A Write the numbers 1 to 10 vertically ↓ on a sheet of paper.
B Draw four vertical | lines. Now the page is divided into three columns. Label these columns 'Yes', 'No', 'I don't know'.
C Work in pairs or groups and write questions 7 to 10 of the questionnaire below:
 1 Do you want to go to university?
 2 Are you going to do the same job your father or mother does?
 3 Will you be rich when you're older?
 4 Will you have to work hard to be rich?
 5 Are you going to get married young?
 6 Do you want to have children when you get married?
 7 . . . .
 8 . . . .
 9 . . . .
10 . . . .

2 Interview 10 other students: ask them the 10 questions and tick their answers on your answer sheet.

3 When you finish, make sentences like these:
Six out of ten students want to go to university.
Three out of ten students think that they are going to be rich.
All the students interviewed want to have children when they get married.

6 The Magic Ring

Structure

FOLLOW MY INSTRUCTIONS AND WRITE DOWN YOUR FINDINGS.

You'll need:
- a sheet of paper to make the rings
- some glue to stick the paper
- a pair of scissors to cut the paper
- a coloured pencil to colour one side of the rings
- a pen to draw lines
- a ruler to draw straight lines

TO TWIST

A TWIST

A TWIST

1 Draw three parallel lines (‖‖) about 4 cm apart down the middle of your sheet of paper.

2 Cut the paper along the lines.
Q1: How many strips of paper have you got?
Q2: How wide (← →) are they?

3 Colour one side (one side only) of the two 4 cm wide strips.

4 Take one of the two strips of paper and stick the ends together to make a ring so that the outside of the ring is coloured and the inside isn't.

5 Take the other strip of paper and twist it once.

6 Stick the ends together so that you can see a coloured end on a white end.

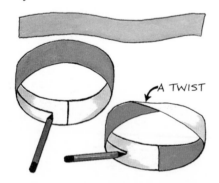

A TWIST

7 Take the first ring you made and draw a line on the inside of the ring until you come back to the point where you started.

8 Do the same with the second ring (the ring with a twist).
Q3: Compare the two rings. Are your lines different? What is the difference?

9 With the scissors, cut along the lines you have just drawn on the two rings.
Q4: What happened to the first ring you made when you cut it?
Q5: What happened to the second ring you made (the ring with a twist)?

10 Draw another line round the ring with a twist.

11 Cut along this line.
Q6: What happened to this ring when you cut it?

Look:
A What do we use the paper for?
B To make the rings.
A What do we use the coloured pencil for?
B To colour one side of the strip.
In pairs, ask and answer questions in the same way about these objects:
a paper
b coloured pencil
c scissors
d pen
e glue
f ruler

Answers:
Q1: Four strips: two 4 cm wide and two more, one on either side of the lines you drew.
Q2: Two of them are 4 cm wide. The width of the other two depends on the size of the sheet of paper you used.
Q3: Yes. On one ring, the line is only on the inside. On the ring with a twist, the line is on both sides!
Q4: It is divided into two rings.
Q5: It didn't divide into two rings: it is still one ring!
Q6: It is now two rings, one inside the other!

24

Have you got a camera?
Do you know how to take photographs?
Have you got a walkman?
Do you know how to take care of your cassettes?

1 Here are two sets of instructions. One is a set of instructions to use a camera and the other is a set of instructions to look after your cassettes properly.
The two sets are mixed up. Can you sort them out?

- Never touch the tape surface
- Hold camera steady
- Focus
- Keep the cassette in the box
- Clean the heads in the cassette player
- Insert film cartridge
- Press button
- Turn the knob until it stops
- Look through the viewfinder
- Do not store in high temperatures

2 Write the instructions in this chart:

How to take care of your cassette tapes	How to use a camera

Joke!

A man ate every night at the same restaurant and the same waiter served him every night. One night, the man paid the bill as usual and then he walked up one wall, across the ceiling, down the other side and out through the window.
The waiter was very surprised. He said, 'That's strange. He usually says good night when he leaves.'

Find the names of the shapes and solids in the pictures in the list of words on the left and underline them:

square

rectangle

triangle

circle

pentagon

diamond

trapeze

cube

sphere

pyramid

cone

cylinder

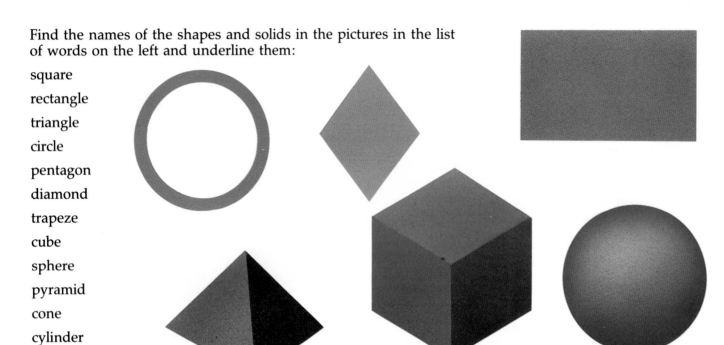

Do you know all the words in the list? Can you think of other shapes and solids?

Mysterious Letters   **Listening**

Episode 4

Sam and Lucy are in Liverpool. They want to find out who wrote their mother some letters many years ago.
Listen to this episode and put the events on the list below in order:

A They asked an old lady for directions.
B They followed a man.
C They walked through the crowd.
D Sam saw a very old building.
E They walked past the school.

F They arrived at the Pier Head.
G They asked a man how to get to the address.
H Sam thanked the man.
I Lucy felt happier.

I Look at the pictures and answer these questions:
a What do we call these objects?
b What do we use them for?

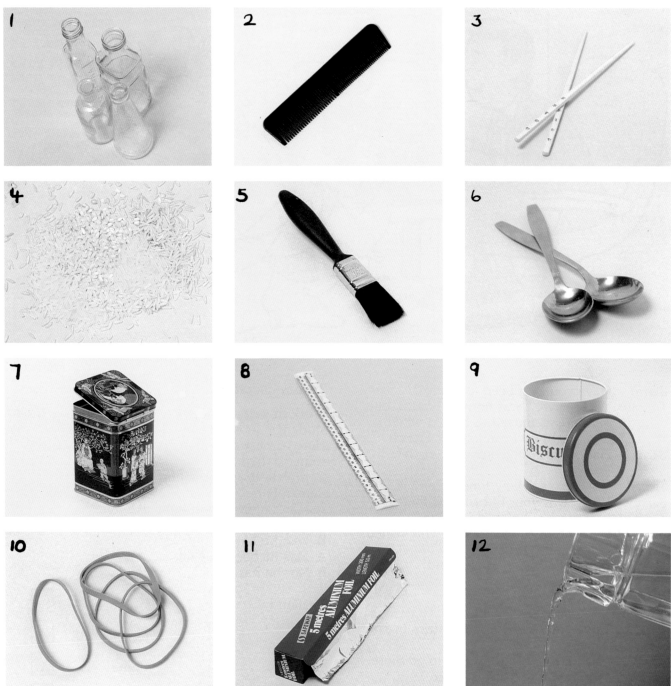

2 We can make musical instruments using these objects. In groups, think of musical instruments you can make using these objects. Make notes. When you finish, you will have to tell the group what instruments you can make and what objects you use to make them.
E.g.: With a metal box and some rice we can make a musical instrument. Put some rice in the box, close it and shake it.

Barry Tobogan has his own chat show. Today he is interviewing Tommy, the famous pop-star.

Barry: Have you ever been to France?

Tommy: Yes, I have. I was born in France, but my parents moved to Britain when I was a baby so I can't speak French.

Barry: Have you played any concerts in France?

Tommy: Yes, I have. Many times.

Barry: When was your last concert there?

Tommy: Last month. I played in Lyon.

Barry: What other countries have you visited?

Tommy: I've visited Thailand.

Barry: When did you visit Thailand?

Tommy: Three years ago.

Barry: Did you like it?

Tommy: Yes, it was fantastic!

Barry: Have you visited any countries in South America?

Tommy: No, I haven't, but I'd like to go there.

Barry: Would you like to play there?

Tommy: I'd love to.

Barry: Will you come to the programme and tell us about South America after your trip?

Tommy: I don't know, Barry. I'm very expensive. Can you afford me?

Barry: I'll start saving now. Ladies and gentlemen . . .Tommy!

Tommy's Trips

Work in pairs. Student A looks at this page and student B looks at page 94 – Tommy's Trips.
Here is a list of countries. Tommy has visited some of them.
Complete the information on the list.
Remember: √ = yes ✗ = no
Ask and answer questions like this:

A Has he been to Thailand?
B Yes, he has.
A Has he been to Chile?
B No, he hasn't.

Thailand	☐	Greece	☐
Chile	☐	Egypt	✔
Germany	✔	China	✗
Turkey	✗	America	☐
Japan	☐	Israel	☐
Colombia	✗	Argentina	☐

Episode 5

Sam and Lucy have found the street of the person who sent their mother some letters many years ago.

'Well sis, here we are.' As they walked along they both counted the door numbers. '60, 58, 56, . . .' 'I don't believe it!' Sam cried, 'there's no number 54! Where's the house?'

There was no number 54, only a space between numbers 52 and 56. Lucy felt very disappointed. 'We've come all this way for nothing!' she said.

Sam thought for a second. 'No, not for nothing. Look Lucy, now that we're here, let's find out what happened to the house. Maybe one of the neighbours can tell us.' He started to march up to the door of the next house.

'But you can't do that!' said Lucy. 'We'll only get into trouble.' 'No, we won't. You'll see,' replied Sam.

Sam rang the bell and a white-haired old man opened the door. 'Yes, young man? What can I do for you?' he said. Sam told him about the letters and about the trip. The old man asked 'Does your mother know you're here?' Lucy shouted 'No!'

The old man looked at them both for a second. Then he said 'Look, let's make a deal. I'll tell you what I know about the house and then you ring your mother.'

Answer these questions:
1 What does Sam call Lucy at the beginning of the episode?
2 Why was Lucy disappointed?
3 What did Sam decide to do?
4 How did Lucy feel about Sam's suggestion?
5 Who answered the door?
6 Was the old man polite or rude?
7 What do you think happened to the house?

1 Before you listen to this song, think of words that sound like:
a train   **c** away
b place   **d** bed

2 Find out what these expressions mean:
a second name
b if you please
c take to your bed
d lose your head

3 Complete the chart below

Infinitive	Simple Past	Past Participle
go	went	gone
	changed	
		kept
take		
	lost	

4 Listen to the song and fill in the blanks:

Mr Woot, Mr Woot,

have you gone away by ....*train*................

have you changed your second ..*name*...........

was it just to cause us ......*pain*................

Mr Woot?

Oh, the town's an empty ....

without your friendly ....

I have always kept a ....

in my heart for you.

Please tell us Mr Woot

why you've gone ....

if you want to come to ....

you ....

if you please, with me.

Mr Woot, Mr Woot,

have you taken to your ....

have you lost your little ....

was it something someone ....

Mr Woot?

Oh, the town's an empty ....

without your friendly ....

I have always kept a ....

in my heart for you.

Please tell us Mr Woot

why you've gone ....

if you want to come to ....

you ....

if you please, with me.

30

7 Opposites

1 Find opposites for these adjectives:
E.g.: happy/unhappy or sad, dirty/clean

1 happy	**6** right	**11** polite	**16** kind
2 dirty	**7** correct	**12** beautiful	**17** friendly
3 large	**8** good	**13** intelligent	**18** true
4 fat	**9** comfortable	**14** slow	**19** easy
5 expensive	**10** young	**15** interesting	**20** late

2 For one of the examples, you found two opposites:
happy/unhappy, sad.
For the other example, you found only one opposite: dirty/clean.
For which adjectives were you able to find two opposites?

3 In the first example, unhappy is a combination of un+happy.
Did you find any other adjectives that form opposites in a similar
way?

A Puzzle

Janet, Mike, Cilla and Joe went to different countries for their
holidays. They travelled by different means of transport.
The countries they visited were: America, France, Mexico, Spain.
The means of transport used were: car, ferry, plane, ship.
Find out who went where and how.
1 Janet didn't go to Mexico.
2 Joe went to Spain.
3 Janet travelled by air.
4 The person who went to France travelled by ferry.
5 The person who travelled by car didn't go to Mexico or America.
6 Cilla travelled by sea.
Write your answers in this chart.

name	country visited	form of transport

1 Read the cartoon strip and answer these questions:
1 What is Mike's problem?
2 Is it a serious problem?
3 Paul gives Mike 3 ideas to help him. What are they?
4 In what 4 different ways does Paul give Mike advice?
5 Do you think that Mike will get the job?

2 Helen and Jonathan are English teenagers. They are studying French in France.
One day, Helen sees that Jonathan's back pocket is full. Helen is curious. She also knows that it is dangerous to carry things in your back pocket.
Here is the dialogue between Helen and Jonathan. Some of Helen's lines are missing. Complete the dialogue using the lines in the box.

H – What have you got in your back pocket?
J – £100.

H – ....
J – Well, I'm going to buy presents for my family. I need the money.

H – ....
J – Yes, I have, but it's got a hole in it.

H – ....
J – I don't know how to mend holes in pockets.

H – ....
J – No, I'm sure he can't mend holes.

H – ....
J – He's got a hole in his trousers. He had it when I arrived in France three weeks ago.

A Why do you say that?
B You shouldn't carry money in your back pocket. Have you got a pocket inside your jacket?
C Oh dear! Why don't you mend it?
D That's a lot of money! If I were you, I wouldn't carry all that money around.
E You can ask your teacher.

1 In many magazines there's a section called "The Problem Page".
People write to the magazine and an expert gives them advice.
Here are some of those letters. Read them and ask your teacher
any words you can't understand.

> *Dear Jane,*
> *My parents don't understand me. I want to have a pet but they tell me that it will make the house dirty. They are so silly! I'm going to leave home.*
> *Angry*

> *Dear Jane,*
> *I'm very embarrassed. I've got very bad breath. I can't get near my friends because I don't want them to smell my bad breath. Can you give me some advice?*
> *Fred*

> *Dear Jane,*
> *I'm very sad because I haven't got any friends. All the students in my class go out together, but they never invite me. Why is this?*
> *Lonely*

> *Dear Jane,*
> *I'm very worried because my hair is falling out. I'm only 19 and I shouldn't have this problem. What can I do?*
> *Worried.*

2 Jane, the expert, wrote these replies, but she forgot to write the
names. Read each reply and write the name of the person it is for.

> **Dear ....**
> Yours is a very common problem and there are many things you can do:
> 1 You should brush your teeth more often.
> 2 You shouldn't eat garlic.
> 3 You should see your dentist.
> Good luck!
> Jane

> **Dear ....**
> You shouldn't do that. It won't solve your problems. Why don't you talk to them? You should tell them how you feel. They'll understand.
> Jane

> **Dear ....**
> You're right, you are very young and you shouldn't have this problem. You should see your doctor. She'll help you.
> Jane

> **Dear ....**
> You sound desperate. Why don't you give a party and invite them to your house? I'm sure things will change.
> Jane

Episode 6

Sam and Lucy arrive at the address they are looking for, but the house isn't there. A neighbour promises to tell them about the house, but he wants them to ring their mother afterwards.

'O.K.' said Lucy and Sam together. 'Well, come in then and sit down.'

Then the old man told them what he knew.

1 Before you listen to the story, answer these questions:
1 What do you think happened to the house?
2 Who do you think wrote those letters?
Discuss your answers with other students. Do you agree? Listen to the story and find out if you're right.

2 Answer these questions:
1 What happened to the house?
2 What is Sam and Lucy's surname?
3 Who wrote the letters?
4 What was Mrs Newman's reaction when she heard where Sam and Lucy were?

The words in this exercise are all related to the things we do in our free time.
In each group of four, find one word that is different from the rest and underline it. E.g.:
cinema – theatre – football – concert

Here, football is the odd one out because it is a sport and all the others are related to art.
In each case, give your reasons why the word you say is the odd one out.

1 jogging – football – rugby – basketball

2 museum – cinema – disco – amusement arcade

3 bird watching – collecting stamps – gardening – train spotting

4 swimming – wind surfing – sailing – jogging

5 painting – writing – reading – sculpting

6 climbing – jogging – tennis – surfing

7 TV – radio – tape recorder – book

8 squash – badminton – football – tennis

What is your favourite pastime?

Project: A Magazine

Activities

Do you read magazines?
Can you think of different types of magazines?
In a magazine there are different sections. Here are some examples:
- Horoscopes
- Book reviews
- Cookery
- Interviews with famous people (e.g. your teacher)
- Top 10 records
- Film reviews

Can you think of any more sections?
Work in groups to write a classroom magazine.
Each group will be in charge of a different section.

These two ornaments look very similar. One is made of silver and the other one is made of a special plastic resin.

The silver ornament is very expensive and it took an artist three months to make it.
The plastic ornament is very cheap and it takes a machine five minutes to make 100.

I What do you think these objects are made of? Discuss your answers with a partner.

2 This is a dialogue between a customer and a shop assistant. Can you find words to substitute for the highlighted words?

C: I'd like a watch, please.
SA: This is a very nice watch.
C: How much is it?
SA: £513.
C: Oh, dear! That's very expensive.
SA: That's because it's made of gold. This one's cheaper. It's made of plastic.
C: How much is the plastic one?
SA: £15.
C: I'll take the plastic one.

3 Write similar dialogues using these words:
a earrings/silver/tin **b** shoes/leather/canvas
c jacket/wool/polyester

Look: a watch is made of gold. **But**: shoes are made of leather.

A man was driving through the country when his car started making a strange noise. The man got out of his car, opened the bonnet and had a look at the engine.

When he was looking at the engine, he heard a voice saying, 'It's the radiator.'

The man looked round and there was a cow standing behind him. The man thought that this was very strange and, feeling a little silly, he asked the cow, 'Did you say something?'

'Yes,' replied the cow. 'I said that it was the radiator making that noise.'

The man couldn't believe his ears! He ran to the nearest town, went into a garage and told them about the speaking cow.

'Was it a brown cow?' asked the car mechanic.

'Yes!' replied the man.

'Well, don't believe anything she told you, she doesn't know anything about cars,' replied the car mechanic.

Answer these questions on the story:

1 What colour was the cow?
2 What was wrong with the car?
3 Why did the man feel a little silly?
4 Why couldn't the man believe his ears?
5 Did the car mechanic think that there was anything strange about the cow?
6 Why did he tell the man not to believe anything the cow told him?

1 All these are names of materials but the letters are not in order. Can you re-order them?

1 saptlic = plastic

2 noir = ...

3 dolg = ...

4 virsel = ...

5 salgs = ...

6 dowo = ...

7 lowo = ...

8 zonber = ...

9 relmab = ...

10 notcot = ...

11 nahic = ...

12 rehalet = ...

13 sanvac = ...

14 klis = ...

2 Find the names of the materials in this square:

```
R D B R O N Z E M I W C
L E A T H E R Y C M Q S
P C O T T O N L S A G M
H A E R W G P V I R O N
K N J W O O L I L B L N
E V F X O R A U K L D Y
S A O C D A S Z I E G L
O S A H Y Q T I B A B O
Z F A I P S I L V E R N
Q X U N P W C T J V I T
N G L A S S O K A B C D
```

Jewellery

Listening

1 Here are some pieces of jewellery. Label them. Ask your teacher any words you don't know.

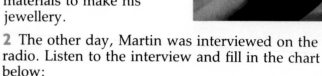

Martin is an artisan. He makes jewellery, but he doesn't use expensive materials – he uses simple materials to make his jewellery.

2 The other day, Martin was interviewed on the radio. Listen to the interview and fill in the chart below:

piece of jewellery	materials used

3 Are you wearing any jewellery? What is it made of?

1 Discuss the following questions with another student:

1 Did you sleep well last night? Why?/Why not?

2 Did you have any dreams?

3 We all dream, but some people cannot remember their dreams. Can you remember your dreams?

If you can remember your dreams, answer questions **4** to **8**.

If you cannot remember your dreams, ask your partner questions **4** to **8**.

4 Can you remember a falling dream?

5 Can you remember a flying dream?

6 Do you dream in colour or in black and white?

7 Can you remember any nightmares?

8 Sometimes we dream about things that happen to us or about a book we're reading or a film we saw. Can you remember any dreams like that?

2 Now you are going to enter a maze. You must read the information on the cards, discuss what to do, take a decision and follow the instructions on the card.

Start the maze on page 84 – A Dream.

The sentences below are incomplete. Fill in the blanks using one (only one) of the four options below each sentence.
E.g.:

Take an umbrella because it . . . . . raining.
a will **b** is **c** go **d** need
The correct answer is **b** so you write **is**.

1 We use a pencil to . . . . . pictures with.
   a draw **b** drawing **c** draws **d** for draw

2 A: I've got two sisters.

   B: . . . . .
   a Neither do I. **b** So do I. **c** So am I. **d** So have I.

3 It's very cold. You . . . . . put on a jacket.
   a need **b** should **c** to **d** shouldn't

4 It's very warm in here. I'm . . . . . open the window.
   a go **b** will **c** going to **d** must

5 You . . . . . brush your teeth every day.
   a must to **b** need **c** have **d** must

6 A: I've got a headache.
   B: . . . . . I get you an aspirin?

   a Shall **b** Mustn't **c** Please **d** Why

7 A: . . . . . you seen this film?
   B: Yes, I have.
   a Did **b** Do **c** Have **d** Will

8 This ring is made . . . . . gold.
   a at **b** of **c** off **d** is

9 You must . . . . . your homework.
   a do **b** doing **c** to do **d** done

10 She . . . . . her homework.
   a has **b** have **c** don't **d** did

1 There is a party at Southford College today. Jack, a boy from Australia, sees a beautiful girl. He introduces himself to her. Here is the dialogue. Some lines are missing. Complete the dialogue using the expressions in the box.
Jack: Hello, I'm Jack. What's your name?
Liz: Hello, Jack. My name's Liz.

1 *Jack:* ....

   Liz: I'm 17.

2 *Jack:* ....

   Liz: I'm American, and you?

3 *Jack:* ....

   Liz: Australian! My sister lives in Australia.
   Jack: Oh! Where does she live?
   Liz: She lives in Sydney.

4 *Jack:* In Sydney! ....

   Liz: Are your parents from Sydney too?
   Jack: Yes, they are.
   (some minutes later . . .)
   Liz: Oh! I love this music.

5 Jack: ....

   Liz: I'd love to.

So do I.
How old are you?
Would you like to dance?
Where are you from?
I'm Australian.

2 The words in these sentences are mixed up. Re-order them.
1 you/could/the/open/please/window/,/?

....

2 money/save/you/some/should.

....

3 camera/you/your/needn't/bring/.

....

4 skirt/is/what/of/this/made/?/

....

5 afternoon/this/rain/will/it/.

....

3 You work for a magazine. You are the expert who writes the replies to the letters on the problem page. Write a reply to this letter:

Dear Expert,
  My parents are angry with me because I failed an exam. I didn't study for this exam because I was very tired and I needed to sleep.
  I can take this exam again and I would like to pass it.
  What do you think I should do?
  John.

41

Goodbye

Riddles

1 What has teeth but cannot eat?

2 What can tell you the time without speaking?

3 What can hear without ears and speak without a mouth?

4 What can you break without touching it?

5 What never asks questions but always gets answered?

6 Why is a golf course like Swiss cheese?

Joke!

A lady went to visit her friend. Her friend was very fat and she had a little daughter. The visitor asked the little girl, 'What will you do when you are as big as your mother?', and the little girl replied, 'I'll diet'.

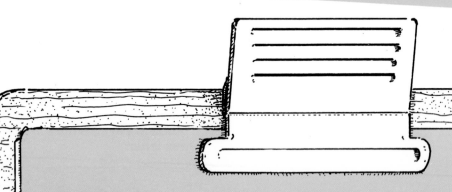

A Quiz

You have spent some time now at your school. You have found out many things about the school and the city or town where the school is. Test your friends. See how much they can remember about the school and the city or the town.

In groups, write a questionnaire (10 questions). When the questionnaires are ready, ask the other groups your questions to test them. Keep a record of the score to see who the winner is.

Answers to the riddles:

1 a comb	4 silence
2 a clock	5 the telephone
3 an echo	6 because it is full of holes

Lap 2

Tommy – heart of gold

1 Listen to the interview and fill in the blanks.

Journalist: You're British, ...?

Tommy: No, I'm not. I'm French. My parents are from France.

Journalist: I see. But they live in Britain,

. . . .?

Tommy: That's right. We live in the same house.

Journalist: You own a big house, ...?

Tommy: Yes, we do. My sisters live in it too.

Journalist: You are a large family, ...?

Tommy: We are. I like living with my family. I've got five sisters and they all look after me.

Journalist: You're a very lucky man! Now Tommy, tell me about your new group. You've formed a new group,

. . . .?

Tommy: Yes, I have. The group's name is 'Tommy and the Cats'. Do you like it?

Journalist: It sounds good. You're planning to

play at Wembley, ...?

Tommy: Yes, we are, and the money will go to

charity. You'll be there, ...?

Journalist: Certainly!

2 The concert at Wembley is about to start. Tommy wants everything to be perfect. He is talking to his manager. Here is what he is saying. Find the correct question tag for each statement.

1 The cameramen are here,
2 You brought my mascot,
3 The Cats have arrived,
4 My girlfriend is here,
5 The lights aren't on,
6 The stage isn't dirty,
7 My guitar is ready,
8 The fans can't see me now,
9 The fans will cheer,
10 The fans won't cause trouble,

a won't they?
b is it?
c isn't she?
d will they?
e aren't they?
f are they?
g didn't you?
h can they?
i isn't it?
j haven't they?

BRAINTEASER
A man leaves his house, walks 1 km South, then he walks 1 km West, then he walks 1 km North and he is back home. Where is his house?

People from other countries think that the British are cold and unfriendly, but this isn't always true. You won't have any problems with your British hosts if you remember a few things:

Greetings:

Always greet people when you haven't seen them for a while.

Say 'Good morning' when you walk into the kitchen or the dining room for your breakfast.

Say 'Good afternoon' when you return home after lunch.

Say 'Good evening' when you get home after 5 p.m.

Say 'Good night' before going to bed.

Meals:

British people don't say anything before a meal, but they are very polite at the table.

If you can't reach the salt cellar say: 'Could you pass the salt, please?'

If the landlady offers you something, say: 'Yes, please' or 'No, thanks'.

Don't forget to say 'Thank you' when they give you your plate.

1 True or false?

a All British people are unfriendly.

b All British people are friendly.

c Some British people are friendly.

d You must greet people every time you see them.

e You have to say 'Good night' before you go to bed.

f You must say 'Thank you' when they give you something to eat.

2 Imagine that a student from Britain is going to stay with a family in your country. Write a list of useful things for this student to remember.

① Top Ten

1. Every week, the 10 most popular songs appear in the 'Top Ten' chart.
Here's this week's chart. Listen to the radio programme and complete it.

2. Write out a list of singers or groups and their songs. Then go round the school asking other students and teachers to vote for their favourite. Finally, write your own 'Top Ten' chart.

Top Ten	
1 The Lizards –	
2	– Nuclear Baby
3 Fabulous Fred –	
4	– Don't go away.
5 Captain G. –	
6	—It's Spring again
7 Fabulous Fred –	
8	– Telegram
9 The Jameson 5 –	
10	– I'm fat

Musical Instruments

1 Match the pictures of the instruments with their names:
1 mouth organ
2 xylophone
3 drums
4 guitar
5 cymbals
6 violin
7 trumpet

2 Classify the instruments into:
a wind instruments
b string instruments
c percussion instruments

This game is very similar to the traditional game of bingo . . . but with a difference: there aren't any numbers on the cards, there are question tags!
Here is an example:

	isn't it?		are they?
can't I?		were you?	

Each student will pick up a card like this one from a pile and he/she will read the sentence on the card:

Look at your card. Have you got a question tag for this sentence? Yes? Then cross out the question tag like this:

	isn't it?		are they?
~~can't I?~~		were you?	

1 Read the cartoon strip and answer these questions:
1 What do Mike and Janet have to do?
2 Can Mike and Janet wear any clothes they want to go to college?
3 Does Tommy have to get up early?
4 What does he have to do?

2 Match the sentences with similar meaning:
a You mustn't eat in class.
b You must speak English.
c You needn't do extra work.
d You need to take notes during the lesson.

1 They make us speak English.
2 We can't study if we don't take notes.
3 They don't make us do extra work.
4 They don't let us eat in class.

3 What do your parents make you do? What do they let you do? Make two lists – one for the things they make you do and the other one for the things they let you do.

4 When you finish writing your lists, compare them with other student's.

Jonathan is an English teenager. He is studying French in France. The other day he wrote a letter to his parents.

1 Read the letter and write a list of things teachers make Jonathan do; a list of things they let him do; a list of things they don't make him do and a list of things they don't let him do.

> Dear Mum and Dad,
>
> I miss you a lot. The school is very nice: there is a very large garden and we can have our lunch there. There is also a gym, a snack bar and a reading room.
>
> There are some rules here: they make us get up early and clean our rooms and they make us study for three hours in the morning, but they let us do what we want in the afternoon.
>
> There are many excursions in the afternoon. They don't make us go on these excursions but I prefer going on excursions to staying at school.
>
> They don't let us go out at night. This is a pity because there's a very good disco in town. But it doesn't matter because we are going to have a disco here next Saturday. On Sundays they let us sleep till late.
>
> I'll say goodbye now
> love Jonathan

2 Write a similar letter to your parents telling them about school.

1 Use these words to fill in the blanks in the sentences below:

annoyed   boring   excited   interested
terrified   amusing   frightened

1 I'm . . . . in computers.

2 This book is . . . . I won't finish reading it.

3 I'm . . . . when I think about nuclear war.

4 The film was very . . . . We laughed from beginning to end.

5 His teacher was . . . . because he was very rude to her.

6 When I saw the monster, I was . . . .

7 I'm going to a concert this evening. I'm very

. . . .

2 Complete the chart. Look at the examples first:

It ...... me.	It's	I'm ....
interests	interesting	interested
bores		
	annoying	
		excited
terrifies		
	amusing	
		frightened

3 Can you think of other words that can go in the chart? Here are some pictures to help you:

1 w _ _ _ _ _ d   **2** t _ _ _ d   **3** p _ _ _ _ _ d

Good Friends   Listening

Episode 1

1 You'll hear the first episode of a story about the four people in the picture. As you listen to it, write down the name and age of each person and what they want to do.

2 What is the relationship between:
a Maggie and Tom?
b Sue and Maggie?
c Paul and Tom?
d Sue and Paul?

Work in pairs. Student A looks at this page. Student B looks at page 94 – An Interview.
You are a reporter. You are going to interview a famous pop star.

1 Work with the other reporters and write out a list of questions you want to ask him/her.
Here is some information about the pop star.
His/her name is Chris Cross.
He/she sings country music.
He/she has got a habit he/she wants to hide . . . (of course you want to find out what it is).
His/her right thumb looks strange . . .
He/she has got a girlfriend/boyfriend but this is a secret. You want to know who the girlfriend/boyfriend is.
He/she is going to give a concert.
He/she never wears fur coats. You want to know why.

2 Interview the pop star.

3 When you have finished, write the article.

Read the story and answer these questions:
1 Why was Jarvis excited on Tuesday?
2 Did Jarvis eat his breakfast as usual?
3 Was he taller than his son?
4 Was he shorter than his sister?

Jarvis Titch woke up very early on Tuesday 11th June. He was very excited: Tuesday was the day when the men from *The Guinness Book of Records* were going to check his height because they thought that he was the smallest man in the world.

Winnie Titch was very excited too. She knew that her husband was small, very small. She imagined her husband on television talking to famous stars. She also imagined herself on T.V. with her husband and their son, Jarvis Jr.

Jarvis ate his breakfast faster than usual, but then he was more excited than usual. The smallest man in the world! His son Jarvis Jr. was smaller than him, but then he was only a boy. He, Jarvis, wasn't as small as his sister Juliette, but then she was a woman, not a man.

The doorbell interrupted his thoughts. 'Here they are!' shouted his wife Winnie, running to open the door. The two men from *The Guinness Book of Records* looked worried. One of them asked, 'How tall is your husband, Mrs Titch?' 'You can ask him yourselves,' replied Winnie and she called her husband. 'Dear, the men from *The Guinness Book of Records* are here. They want to ask you something.'

STOP READING NOW
What do you think will happen next?

Listen to the end of the story and fill in the blanks:

'I'm three foot two,' said Jarvis . . . . the men asked him. 'You can . . . . it. Have you got a measuring . . . .?'

'That won't be necessary, Mr Titch . . . . Tiny phoned us this morning. He . . . . three foot one. You are taller . . . . him. He is the shortest man . . . . the world,' replied one of the . . . . from *The Guinness Book of Records*.

. . . . felt a pain in his chest . . . . he fell to the floor. Winnie . . . . for an ambulance, but it was . . . . late: Jarvis was dead.

The undertaker . . . . after the doctor to measure poor . . . . He had to have a coffin . . . . to measure. The two men from . . . . *Guinness Book of Records* were there. . . . . were very sad.

'I can't find . . . . measuring tape,' said the undertaker.

'Here, ... can use mine,' said Winnie.

'No, ... never use that kind of tape. . . . . is very unreliable. It usually gives . . . . incorrect measurement,' replied the undertaker.

After . . . . few minutes, the undertaker found his . . . . measuring tape.

'Let's see, three foot . . . . I've never seen a body as . . . . as your husband's Mrs Titch.'

When . . . . two men from *The Guinness Book . . . . Records* saw Winnie's face, they ran . . . . of the house as fast as . . . . could.

I Answer these questions about the second part of the story:
1 Why did Jarvis have to have a coffin made to measure?
2 Why didn't the undertaker want to use Winnie's measuring tape?
3 Who was smaller, Mr Tiny or Jarvis?

2 Read through the story again and fill in the blanks:

1 They thought that he was . . . . in the world.

2 Jarvis ate his breakfast . . . . usual.

3 He was more . . . . than usual.

4 His son Jarvis was . . . . him.

5 He wasn't . . . . his sister Juliette.

6 Mr Tiny is three foot one. You are . . . . him.

7 He is the . . . . man in the world.

8 I've never seen a body . . . . your husband's.

Episode 2

On Tuesday afternoon, Sue left her house early because she wanted to get to college early. She wanted to borrow a book from the college library. It was a lovely summer's day, so she decided to walk through the park.

As she was walking through the park, she saw Tom talking to another girl. Sue was very surprised. The other woman looked older than Tom. Besides, Tom was Maggie's boyfriend and Maggie was her best friend.

Sue felt very sad, but she didn't know what to do. Talk to Tom? Tell Maggie? Sue was very confused, so she ran to college as fast as she could.

At the library, she met Paul and she told him about Tom and the other girl.

'What can I do?' she asked. 'Maggie will be very upset when she finds out and I don't want to upset Maggie, but she's my best friend. I must do something!'

'No,' said Paul, 'you shouldn't tell her, you mustn't interfere.'

'But she'll find out, won't she?' asked Sue.

'You're going to the party on Saturday, aren't you?' asked Paul.

'Yes, I am,' replied Sue.

'Wait until the party. Give Tom time to tell Maggie himself,' was Paul's advice to Sue.

'O.K.' said Sue, 'but I won't give Tom any more time. He has to be honest.'

Answer these questions:
1 Why did Sue want to go to college early on Tuesday?
2 Why did she decide to walk through the park?
3 Why did she feel sad?
4 Do you think Paul's advice was good?
5 Do you think Tom will tell Maggie about the other woman?
6 What do you think will happen next?

Do you know the names for the different parts of the body? Look at the picture and write the numbers in the boxes next to the words.

ankle	☐	head	☐
arm	☐	knee	☐
chest	☐	leg	☐
chin	☐	mouth	☐
ear	☐	neck	☐
elbow	☐	nose	☐
eye	☐	shoulder	☐
finger	☐	stomach	☐
foot	☐	toe	☐
forehead	☐	tooth	☐
hair	☐	waist	☐
hand	☐	wrist	☐

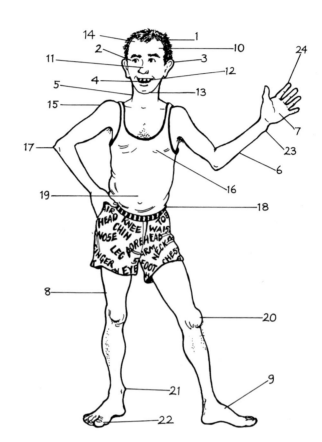

A Survey: A shopping centre   Activities

1 Where can you buy:
sweets?	**a** stationer's
magazines?	**b** newsagent's
records?	**c** supermarket
pen and paper?	**d** record shop
aspirins?	**e** baker's
cakes?	**f** chemist's

(Some of the things you can buy at more than one shop.)

2 Go to the nearest shopping centre and write a list of the shops you find there.

3 There are things you can buy at the supermarket and at other shops, e.g.: you can buy bread at the supermarket and at the baker's. Write out a list of those things and the shops where you can buy them, apart from the supermarket.

4 Find out the prices for the things on your list at the supermarket and at the other shops.

5 Compare the prices. Write sentences like these: 'A bar of chocolate is cheaper at the supermarket than it is at the newsagent's.' 'A packet of tissues isn't as expensive at the chemist's as it is at the supermarket.'

The snaps came out blurred because you moved the camera.
In future, remember:

If you move the camera, the snaps will come out blurred.

The snaps are dark because there wasn't enough light.
In future, remember:

If there isn't enough light, the snaps will come out dark.

Your friend hasn't got a head! You didn't look through the viewfinder.
In future, remember:

If you don't look through the viewfinder, your friend may lose his head.

Answer these questions:
1 What will happen if you move the camera?
2 What is necessary to take clear snaps?
3 What may happen to your friend if you don't focus correctly?
Can you give some more advice?

What will . . .?

Work in pairs. Student A asks the first 4 questions and student B finds the answers. Then student B asks the last 4 questions and student A finds the answers.

Questions:
1 What will happen if you don't study?
2 Is he going to buy the bicycle?
3 Will you help me?
4 What will you do if it stops raining?
5 What will happen if he comes late?
6 Will they go on holiday?
7 What will happen if I don't speak English?
8 Are you going to see her?

Answers:
a I'll go to the park.
b The teacher will be angry.
c I'll fail the exam.
d If I have time.
e If they've got the money.
f You'll forget it.
g If it's cheap.
h If you ask me to.

There are thousands of different species of plants, insects and animals. They are all important.

Some species depend on others to survive. If one species disappears, another species may suffer.

For example, the beautiful panda eats only bamboo shoots. It can only live in certain areas: those areas where bamboo grows. Sadly, the people who live in those areas want to plant other things, so they burn the bamboo. The panda now has very little food. If the bamboo disappears completely, the panda won't have anything to eat. It will die. Another species may suffer if the panda disappears.

This is a "chain". It is a short chain. There are longer chains. For example, butterflies need flowers to live and birds eat butterflies. Some birds may not find enough food if butterflies disappear, so indirectly birds depend on flowers to survive.

It is not easy to predict what may happen if one species disappears so we must be very careful not to destroy the natural balance.

Answer these questions:
1 What may happen if the panda disappears?
2 What will happen if the people continue burning the bamboo?
3 What is a "chain"?
4 Can you think of other chains?
5 Can you think of a chain that may affect us?

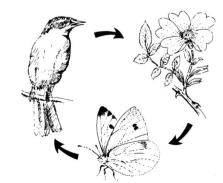

Are you happy? If you aren't happy, this song will make you feel happy. If you are happy, this song won't make you feel sad. Listen to the song and write the missing words in the blanks:

If the . . . . shines

I'll go to the . . . .

If it . . . . to rain

I'll stay in . . . .

If my love . . . .

I'll sing . . . . a bird

If he doesn't . . . .

I'll sing all the . . . .

Oh, life's . . . . right

When you sing a . . . .

Just sing . . . .

The Conditional Rap

If I . . . . the bus

I'll wait for the . . . .

If I . . . . a vase

I won't get . . . .

If the wind . . . .

I'll set . . . . to sail

If I don't rob a . . . .

I . . . . go to jail.

Oh, life's . . . . right

When you sing a . . . .

Just sing . . . .

The Conditional Rap

If you . . . . along

I'll hum . . . . tune

If you . . . . sing

The flowers . . . . bloom

Come on and be . . . .

Just . . . . a song

If you . . . . sing

You won't live . . . .

Oh, life's . . . . right

If you sing a . . . .

Just sing . . . .

The Conditional Rap

58

All these words are related to photography but the letters are not in order. Put the letters in order and then label the picture writing the words in the boxes.

1 remaca = ...

2 milf = ...

3 snel = ...

4 fahls = ...

5 thilg = ...

6 diferwevin = ...

7 socuf = ...

8 hotos = ...

9 pasn = ...

10 lorl = ...

A Maze – Explorer **Activities**

1 Match the words with their definitions:

a explorer	**1**	Very small fish that can eat a cow in seconds.
b piranhas	**2**	A kind of boat.
c canoe	**3**	A very dry place.
d tiger	**4**	A river animal with a big mouth.
e canyon	**5**	A wild animal that is related to the cat.
f bridge	**6**	A very hot and very green place.
g head hunter	**7**	A primitive house.
h crocodile	**8**	A deep space between mountains.
i jungle	**9**	People who make other people's heads smaller.
j desert	**10**	A person who investigates new places.
k hut	**11**	A way of getting across a river without getting wet.

2 Now you are going to enter a maze. You must read each card, discuss what to do next, decide what to do next and follow the instructions on the cards very carefully. Start the maze on page 84 – Explorer.

5 Let's go...!

I Read the cartoon strip and answer these questions:
1 Why are Mike and Paul bored?
2 Paul has an idea. What is it?
3 Why doesn't Mike want to go to the cinema?
4 What is Mike's first suggestion?
5 Why doesn't Paul like picnics?
6 What does he prefer to do?
7 What is Mike's second suggestion?
8 Why can't they go to the concert?

PAUL IS A FRIEND OF MIKE'S. THEY BOTH GO TO SOUTHFORD COLLEGE. THEY AREN'T AT COLLEGE TODAY BECAUSE IT'S A HOLIDAY.

I'm bored. What can we do?

Let's go to the cinema. They're showing 'The Unteachables'.

No, I've seen that film. Besides the weather's so nice! I don't want to sit indoors.

Well, what do you suggest?

Why don't we go for a picnic with the girls?

No. I don't like picnics. The ants eat more than you do in the end.

I know! We can go to Tommy's Concert at Wembley!

That's a great idea!

Only... the tickets are very expensive.

I'm bored. What can we do?

2 Work in pairs. Ask and answer questions like this:
A: It's a holiday tomorrow. What can we do?
B: Let's go to the cinema.
    or: Why don't we visit Janet?
A: That's a good idea!
    or: No, I'd rather go to the park.

Use these questions:
a It's a holiday tomorrow. What can we do?
b It's Janet's birthday next week. What can we buy her?
c Mike's sad. How can we cheer him up?
d Where can we go for our holidays?
e It's late. How can we get to college on time?
f Our house is on fire. What can we do?

Lewis Carroll wrote a book, Alice in Wonderland. In this book there is a poem. Here is the poem:

"Fury said to
a mouse, That
he met in the
house, 'Let
us both go
to law: *I*
will prose-
cute *you.*—
Come, I'll
take no de-
nial: We
must have
the trial;
For really
this morn-
ing I've
nothing
to do.'
Said the
mouse to
the cur.
'Such a
trial, dear
Sir. With
no jury
or judge,
would
be wast-
ing our
breath.'
'I'll be
judge.
I'll be
jury,'
said
cun-
ning
old
Fury:
'I'll
try
the
whole
cause,
and
con-
demn
you to
death.'"

1 Can you guess its title?
Hint: The title of the poem is its shape

Read the poem with the help of a dictionary.

Listen to the tape and find the words that rhyme in the poem.

2 Here is a poem I wrote. It is also a shape poem. In my poem there is no rhyme.

Find a title for my poem.

3 Write a shape poem. Snakes are an easy shape.

Some words in English sound the same and have the same spelling, but they don't mean the same. E.g.: "fan" can be a supporter of a football team or it can be an object we switch on when it's too warm and we want some cold air.

Some words in English sound the same but they have different spelling and meaning. E.g.: "read", the Simple Past tense of the verb "to read" and "red", the colour.

1 Can you find pairs of words that sound the same but that have the two different meanings listed below?

a Simple Past tense of the word to blow; a colour

b intelligent; full of light

c to put pen to paper; opposite of 'wrong'

d an ache; the glass part of a window

e a type of competition; a type of people

f a country; porcelain

g to hit; what we do to eggs when we make an omelette

h a story; the long part at the back of a mouse, or other animal

i a letter of the alphabet; a type of drink

j opposite of 'strong'; 7 days

2 What pairs have different spelling?

3 Do you like jokes? The next exercise is about jokes. Work in pairs. Student A looks at page 92 – Did you say 'right' or 'write'? – and student B looks at page 95 – Did you say 'right' or 'write'?

Episode 3

Listen to the episode and decide whether the following statements are true or false:
1 Sue was nice to Tom.
2 Tom stopped talking to Sue.
3 Sue asked Tom for a drink.
4 Tom offered Maggie a drink.
5 Maggie thought that Sue was unfriendly to Tom.
6 Maggie's words made Sue feel sad.
7 Maggie thought that Sue had problems.
8 Sue said 'goodbye' to Maggie before she left.
Can you remember any words from the passage that express feelings?

Suggestions   Activities

You are going to work in pairs. Student A looks at page 93 and student B looks at this page.

1 Suggest things to do:

2 Student A will suggest activities. Read the information below and respond accordingly.
– You enjoy meeting new friends
– You think concerts are boring and you don't like crowds
– You think 'Space Invaders' is a stupid game
– You hate dancing
– You think that excursions are not very interesting

Lynn and Mark Stowe are brother and sister. They are athletes. They are training for the next Olympic Games. They started training 6 months ago.

Hannah is travelling round the world. She started travelling in December.

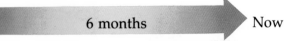

6 months   Now

December   Now

How long have you been training?

We've been training for 6 months

NOW YOU ANSWER

How long has she been travelling?

Work in pairs. Student B looks at page 94 – Two Famous People and student A looks at this page.

Two Famous People

You have got some information about Shamrock Holes. Student B will ask you for this information. Answer his/her questions. When he/she has finished you have to ask him/her for information about Tommy.

Shamrock Holes has been investigating crimes for 20 years. He moved to Liverpool 12 years ago. When he was a child, he started collecting postcards. Last year, he started studying Astronomy.

Tommy
Ask questions like this:
How long has he been ....?

singing with the Cats ....?

collecting sunglasses ....?

living in Southford ....?

going to singing lessons ....?

Episode 4

Read the episode and answer these questions:
1 Why was Sue angry?
2 What did Paul think of the other woman?
3 Why didn't Paul hear Sue's complaint?
4 How did Tom and the other woman leave the hall?
5 Whose car did Tom and the other woman drive away in?
6 How did Sue decide to follow them?
7 What did she say to the taxi driver?
8 What did the taxi driver think of Sue's command?
9 How much did Sue pay the driver?
10 What do you think will happen next?

Sue was very angry. Maggie thought that she, her best friend, was unfriendly. And all this trouble just because Tom was seeing another girl. And . . . there she was! And Tom was talking to her! Sue had to talk to someone. 'Where is Paul?' she asked herself.

'There's the other woman,' Sue said to Paul when she found him.

'What other woman?' asked Paul.

'You know, the one Tom is seeing,' Sue replied impatiently.

'Oh, yes. She's very pretty!' exclaimed Paul.

'You men are all the same!' complained Sue, but Paul didn't hear her because he was talking to another friend.

Sue was furious. How could Paul be so silly! But, where were Tom and the other girl? She looked around the hall and she saw them leaving through a side door.

Sue made up her mind to follow them. She ran out of the hall just in time to see Tom and the other girl driving away in Tom's car so she hailed a taxi.

'Follow that car!' she told the taxi driver.

'You've watched too many detective films,' said the driver laughing, and he followed Tom's car.

They drove across the town until they got to an abandoned house.

'Well, here we are, young lady,' said the driver. 'The car we followed is over there. That'll be £10, please.' Sue paid the taxi driver and walked up to the house.

This is a song about the things we want to do but that we never do.
This person has been dreaming much too long.
Before you listen to the song, match the words in the column on the left with the definitions in the column on the right.

1 to share —   **a** not in prison

2 to plan   **b** not in the city, in nature

3 to wonder   **c** to use with someone else

4 wild   **d** to think carefully about the future

5 free   **e** to ask myself

6 somewhere   **f** some place

7 trip   **g** a journey

8 breathe   **h** to take air in and then to let it out

Listen to the song and fill in the blanks:

I've been . . . .

I've been . . . . of getting . . . .

somewhere;

as long as it is my . . . . place

and I don't have to . . . .

I've been . . . . much too long

I've been . . . .

I've been . . . . to get a . . . .

somewhere

as . . . . as there is space outside

and you can . . . . the air;

I've been . . . . much too long

I've been . . . .

I've been . . . . about taking a

. . . . somewhere;

. . . . long . . . . it is wild and

free

and there . . . . no one there;

I've been . . . . much too long

I've been . . . .

I've been . . . . about putting it down in

a . . . .

as long as it's not . . . . long

and you . . . . hum along;

I've been . . . . much too long.

1 The pictures below, combined, make up words. Can you find those words?

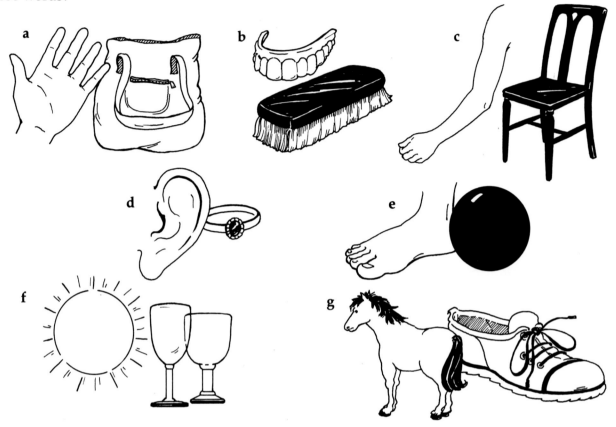

2 Can you think of other English words which are two words put together?

A Picture – A Story

Activities

Work in pairs. Student B looks at page 96 – A picture – a story. Student A looks at this page.

Student B is going to describe a picture to you. You must find out the story behind the picture. To find out the story, you'll have to ask student B questions but student B can only answer 'yes' or 'no'.

Have you guessed the story? Now you are going to describe a picture to student B and student B will ask you many questions to find out the story behind your picture. You can only anwer 'yes' or 'no'.

Read the description of the picture out to student B.
picture: There is a man in a box, laughing.

Don't tell student B the story, but read it in silence.
story: the box is a telephone box and the man is laughing because his friend has just told him a joke.

Cilla: What do you mean 'what for'? Wouldn't you like to have a lot of money?

Janet: Not really. What would you do if you had a lot of money?

Cilla: If I had a lot of money, I'd travel round the world.

Janet: Yes, that would be nice.

Cilla: No, I know – I'd like to be famous too.

Janet: Rich *and* famous!

Cilla: Yes! What would you do if you were rich?

Janet: Mmm . . . If I were rich . . . If I had a lot of money . . . I'd . . . I'd . . . I wouldn't know what to do with my money. I suppose that if I had a lot of money I'd put it in the bank.

Cilla: In the bank!?!? I wouldn't put it in the bank. I'd spend it.

Janet: You'll never be rich then.

1 True or false?

1 Cilla is very rich.

2 Janet isn't rich.

3 Cilla would travel round the world if she were rich.

4 Janet would spend all her money if she were rich.

5 Janet doesn't think that Cilla can be rich.

6 Cilla thinks that Janet is silly.

Look:

The radio was out of order yesterday.

The radio is still out of order today.

If the radio weren't out of order, I'd send a message.

2 Think of an animal you would like to be but don't tell anyone! Think of things the animal would do every day.

Now on a piece of paper, write: *If I were an X, I'd* . . . and make a list of the things you would do – but don't tell anyone what your animal is! In pairs or groups, read out your list, beginning with – If I were an X, I'd . . . and try to guess all the animals.

Episode 5

Sue was very frightened, but she had to find out what was happening. She pushed the front door open. It creaked. She walked into the house and the wind slammed the door shut again. She turned round and tried to open the door but she couldn't.

As she was trying to open the door, she felt a heavy hand on her shoulder.

'What are you looking for?' asked a voice. Sue turned round. A very tall man was holding her shoulder. He had asked the question.

'I . . . I . . . I followed a friend of mine here a . . . a . . . and . . . '

Sue tried to sound calm but she couldn't.

'Do you think I'm going to believe that?' interrupted the man.

'Well, I . . .' Sue tried to speak but the man didn't give her time to finish. He took her to another room.

Sue was very surprised to see Tom, the other woman and an older man talking in the room.

'Tom!' shouted Sue.

'Sue!' said Tom who was even more surprised to see Sue there.

'What are you doing here?'

'I followed you, but what's going on?' asked Sue.

'Sorry Sue,' said Tom, 'I haven't got time to tell you.' Then he said to the tall man: 'Take her to a safe room and lock her in.'

'Wait, Tom!' Sue tried to protest but the tall man took her upstairs.

1 Here is a list of events. Put them in the order in which they happened:

a Sue tried to sound calm
b The wind slammed the door shut
c Tom was surprised to see Sue
d Sue was surprised to see Tom
e The tall man took Sue to see Tom
f The tall man took Sue to a safe place
g Sue opened the door
h Sue couldn't open the door

2 Find two words in the passage that describe noises.

Some verbs, combined with a certain preposition have a special meaning.
Some verbs always go with the same preposition.
Can you complete the sentence below using the correct preposition?
Use **up, down, on, off, with, about, at, for, to**

a It's very cold. I'll put . . . . my pullover.

b Don't forget to take . . . . your watch before you get into the water.

c There's a very good programme on T.V. now. Could you switch it . . . ., please?

d I get . . . . at 7 o'clock every day.

e Wake . . . .! It's 7 o'clock!

f Look . . . . that man! He's going to fall.

g I like listening . . . . music.

h Speak . . . .! I can't hear you.

i Next month I'll go back . . . . my country.

j I'm looking . . . . my glasses. Have you seen them?

k 'This book is boring.' 'I agree . . . . you.'

l Shut . . . .! You're talking too much.

m When I think . . . . my holidays, I feel happy.

n Stand . . . . and give your seat to that old lady.

o I'm so tired. I need to sit . . . .

p You have to buy your ticket when you get . . . . the bus.

q Ring the bell, please. We have to get . . . . at the next stop.

A Puzzle

Activities

Work in pairs to solve this puzzle:
Mary, Mike, Jack and Susan have to get the school hall ready for the disco night.
They have a lot to do: wash the curtains, clean the windows, tidy the room and dust the furniture. They all do their tasks at different times: 2 o'clock, 3 o'clock, 4 o'clock and 5 o'clock.

Can you find out who did what when?
1 The curtains were washed by one of the girls, but not at 2.00.
2 Mike finished his job at 2.30.
3 Some water, a cloth and some soap were used to do the job at 5.00.
4 Susan tidied the room.
5 The curtains were washed one hour before the room was tidied.

Write your answers in a chart.

This song doesn't talk about the way things really are. It talks about an unreal world.

1 Before you listen to the song, match the words that sound similar.

1 champagne	a mechanical	1 b, c, i...
2 ice-cream	b pain	2 ....
3 name	c same	3 ....
4 me	d dream	4 ....
5 understand	e before	5 ....
6 war	f see	6 ....
7 practical	g absurd	7 ....
8 world	h galore	8 ....
9 fools	i rain	9 ....
10 chimpanzees	j man	10 ....
11 game	k trees	11 ....
12 poor	l along	12 ....
13 song	m schools	13 ....

2 Listen to the song and fill in the blanks:

If all the land were . . . .

and all the sea . . . .

then life would be one long sweet . . . .

and death would have no . . . .

There would be no problems, there'd be no

. . . .

We'd eat and drink and dance all day,

at night we'd do the . . . .

If I were you and you were . . . .

maybe we'd . . . .

why people find it hard to . . . .

a man is just a . . . .

There'd be no frontiers, there'd be no

. . . .

There'd be one crazy little . . . .

that's never been . . . .

If we were more . . . .

and robots ruled the . . . .

life would be . . . .

and maybe quite . . . .

There would be no wise men, there'd be no

. . . .

We all would bleep like robot sheep,

programmed in robot . . . .

If banks were homes for . . . .

and work were just a . . . .

If dollar bills grew up like . . . .

and diamonds fell like . . . .

there'd be no unemployed, there'd be no

. . . .

we'd drive around in limousines

eating caviare . . . .

If I didn't think so much
maybe I'd understand
If I didn't drink so much
I'd be a happy man
If I didn't sing so much, maybe I'd write good songs
and maybe you would sing with me or just try to hum along

71

Choose the correct answer for the following questions:

1 *Mona Lisa* was painted by
  a Leonardo Da Vinci
  b El Greco
  c Picasso

2 Coffee is produced in
  a Sweden
  b Brazil
  c England

3 'Yesterday' was sung by
  a Madonna
  b Wet Wet Wet
  c The Beatles

4 Gunpowder was invented by
  a the Chinese
  b the British
  c the Egyptians

5 America was discovered in
  a 1942
  b 1294
  c 1492

6 Australia was discovered by
  a Christopher Columbus
  b Marco Polo
  c Captain Cook

7 Television was invented
  a in the 18th century
  b in the 19th century
  c in the 20th century

8 The Beatles were born in
  a Texas
  b Liverpool
  c Quebec

9 Charlie Chaplin was born in
  a America
  b France
  c Britain

10 The telephone was invented by
  a Einstein
  b Bell
  c Edison

We are told at school that Christopher Columbus and his crew were the first people to sail across an ocean but some experts think that this is not strictly true.

Read the article below and find out what the experts think.

This beautiful boat is the Uro. It is not made of wood or glass fibre. It is made of reeds.

It took Mr Paulino Esteban two months to build the hull from 2800 bundles of reeds cut from Lake Titicaca in the Andes.

The cabin is made of bamboo. No nails were used to build the Uro. This is the way the old Andean people built their boats.

The Uro sailed from Peru to New Zealand in 1988 to prove that it is possible that people from the Andes sailed to Asia long before America was discovered by Columbus.

In 1947, Mr Thor Heyerdal travelled from Peru to Polynesia in a raft called Kontiki made of balsa wood to prove that this theory is possible.

Write questions for these answers about the article:
1 Mr Paulino Esteban
2 Two months
3 It was made of balsa wood
4 It is made of bamboo
5 In 1947
6 From Lake Titicaca in the Andes.

This was one of the most famous groups in the world. Some
people say that they were the greatest.
Listen to this section of a radio programme on pop music and fill
in the chart below.

	John	George	Paul	Ringo
full name				
date of birth				
instrument played				
other information				

Write *was* or *were* in the boxes and fill in the blanks with a verb from the list below. Put the verbs into the passive form.

1 *La Traviata* is an opera. It [   ] . . . . by Verdi.

2 America [   ] . . . . by Columbus.

3 *E.T.* is a film. It [   ] . . . . by Spielberg.

4 The new hospital [   ] . . . . by the Queen.

5 We [   ] . . . . at the airport.

6 The pyramids [   ] . . . . by the Egyptians.

7 The house [   ] . . . . by a professional decorator.

8 Rice [   ] . . . . in China 1000 years ago.

9 'Message in a bottle' [   ] . . . . by The Police.

10 The telephone [   ] . . . . by Graham Bell.

11 The *Mona Lisa* [   ] . . . . by da Vinci.

12 My watch [   ] . . . . in Switzerland.

13 *Romeo and Juliet* [   ] . . . . by Shakespeare.

14 The excursions [   ] . . . . by our group leaders.

15 The 1986 World Cup [   ] . . . . by Argentina.

compose	discover
win	write
decorate	invent
grow	direct
make	organize
meet	sing
paint	build
open	

Project: A Radio Programme   Activities

Can you think of different types of radio programmes? Some programmes are divided into different sections. Here is a list of possible sections:

Book Review
Top Ten
Letters to the editor

Interviews with famous people
  (e.g. your teacher)
Cookery
Topics of General Interest

Can you think of other sections?
Work in groups to prepare a radio programme.
Each group is in charge of a different section.

1 Read this cartoon strip and find out if these statements are true or false.

a Laura is married to Janet's brother.
b Janet had an accident in the sea.
c Mike saved Janet's life.
d Janet's boyfriend is in Canada.
e Janet is sad.
f Mike introduced his friends to Janet.

Look: He's a lifeguard. He saved my life.
He's the lifeguard who saved my life.

Look: He's a boy. I love him.
He's the boy I love.

2 Mike is showing Janet some photographs. Join the sentences he says in the same way as above:

1 She is a teacher. She taught me Maths.
2 This is a beach. My parents take me there every year.
3 He is a cousin. He travelled round the world.
4 She is a girl. I went out with her last year.
5 She is a girl. I'm going to invite her to the cinema tomorrow.
6 She is one of my sisters. She lives in Spain.
7 He is one of my uncles. I like him best.

Riddles!

a What has teeth but cannot eat?
b What can hear without ears and can answer you without a mouth?
c What has a face without eyes and has hands without fingers?

Wimbledon is a beautiful suburb of London. It is famous all over the world for the tennis tournaments which are played there every summer.

Some of the players that take part in the tournament are also famous all over the world. You probably know some of them.

◁ This is Bjorn Borg. He's the man who won the Wimbledon Men's Championship many times.

John McEnroe is the one who shouted at the umpires. ▷

◁ This is Martina Navratilova. She's the woman who won the Wimbledon Women's Championship many times.

This is Joe Bloggs. He is a man who has never won any championships, but he is a man who enjoys playing tennis ▷ all year round.

Answer these questions:
1 Who are the players who won the Wimbledon Championship many times?
2 Who is the player who was very bad tempered?
3 Is Joe Bloggs famous?
4 Can you think of any other famous tennis players?

1 Look at the pictures. You'll hear some sounds related to the pictures. Number the pictures in the order in which you hear the sounds.

2 These are words to describe those sounds. Put them in the order in which you heard them.
a slam
b jangle
c sigh
d creak
e knock
f screech

3 Write a definition for each word. E.g.: 'Slam is the noise made by a door closing.' or 'Slam is the sound made by a door closing.'

4 In pairs or groups make up a story using the sounds in the order in which you heard them.

Good Friends

Listening

Episode 6

This is the last episode. What do you think is going to happen?
Discuss your answer with other students.

Listen to the last episode and find out if you were right.

Listen to the episode again and list all the words you hear which describe noises.

Answer these questions:
1 How did Sue feel when she heard all the noises?
2 How did she feel when she saw Tom?
3 Who was the other woman?

Have you ever played bingo?
Do you know how to play it?
This is bingo but it is different. 1. The numbers are names. 2. To complete your card you must write the person's job under the name. 3. Every student will read out names and jobs.
Here is an example:
There will be a pile of cards like this one:

Miss Harrison

catch/thieves

Each student will pick up a card from the pile and read the information out like this:

Miss Harrison is the one who catches thieves

You will have a card like this one:

Harrison job:		Green job:	
	Wright job:		Monk job:

When you hear one of the names on the card and the description of the job, you write the name of the job in the correct box like this:

Harrison job: *policewoman*		Green job:	
	Wright job:		Monk job:

The sentences below are incomplete. Fill in the blanks using one (only one) of the four options below each sentence.
E.g.:

    Take an umbrella because it . . . . raining
    a will **b** is **c** go **d** need
    The correct answer is **b** so you write **is**.

1 Tommy's a singer, ... ?

a haven't he **b** was he **c** isn't he **d** can he

2 My parents . . . . get up early.

a let **b** me **c** make I **d** make me

3 If it . . . . , I'll go to the cinema.

a rains **b** raining **c** will rain **d** rained

4 How long . . . . ?

a been training **b** been trained **c** have you been training **d** have

you training

5 Our house isn't . . . . yours.

a bigger as **b** as bigger as **c** as big than **d** as big as

6 What would you do if . . . . £1000?

a you have **b** you had **c** had you **d** you has

7 *Hamlet* . . . . Shakespeare.

a was written by **b** was wrote by **c** was written **d** were written

by

8 This is a picture of the athlete . . . . the race yesterday.

a who win **b** who won **c** won **d** who

9 A: I'm tired.

   B: You . . . . go to bed.

a should to **b** why don't **c** should **d** do let

10 I have been saving money . . . . six months.

a ago **b** for **c** when **d** at

1 Sandy and Jill are friends. They are not at school because today is a holiday. They are discussing what to do. Here is the dialogue, but some of the lines are missing. Complete the dialogue using the expressions in the box.

Sandy: What can we do this afternoon?

Jill: ....
Sandy: No, I don't like walking in the park. There are too many insects.

Jill: ....
Sandy: That's a great idea . . . but I haven't got any money to buy the ticket.

Jill: ....
Sandy: Well, why don't we visit Mike?

Jill: ....
Sandy: I know! Let's go to the swimming pool.

Jill: ....
Sandy: Don't worry, I can lend you one of mine.
Jill: O.K. Let's go.

Why don't we go to the cinema?

No, Mike lives miles away from here.

What do you suggest?

I haven't got a swimming costume

Let's go for a walk in the park

2 The words in these sentences are mixed up. Re-order them.

1 for/bus/waiting/the/you/been/long/have/how/?

....

2 been/since/o'clock/I've/waiting/2/.

....

3 so/sweets/many/shouldn't/you/eat/.

....

4 let's/my/me/use/sister/bicycle/her/.

....

5 boots/leather/these/of/are/made/.

....

3 A friend of yours wants to come to your school, but first she wants to have some information about the school. Write her a letter describing the school and telling her about the things they let you do or the things they make you do here.

Goodbye

Shamrock Holes and the Flying Security Guards

Read the story, fill in the blanks and solve the mystery!

Shamrock Holes is a very good[1]........ so people from all over the[2]........ write to him to ask him to investigate[3]........ cases.

Here is one he investigated[4]........ week:

The caretaker of a small[5]........... in Texas went to work on[6]........ 15th of June at 6 a.m. as[7]........ When he got to the bank,[8]........ found the two security guards tied[9]........ ropes round their waists to a[10]........ in the ceiling. He helped them down and then dried the floor [11]........ it was very wet.

The guards[12]........ him this: 'During the night, a[13]........ of thieves came, hung us from[14]........ beam and then stole the money.' Shamrock Holes told the sherrif to arrest the two guards because they were the thieves. The sheriff arrested the guards and they confessed. How did Shamrock Holes know this?

Use these words:
the	difficult	get	detective
he	gang	Monday	told
beam	last	world	with
because	usual	bank	

Test your friends: write your own quiz

Some of you have done all the book. Some of you have done part of it. I hope you've learnt a lot and enjoyed yourselves.

How much can you remember?

Work in groups and prepare a questionnaire on the characters in this book.

When the questionnaires are ready, ask the other groups your questions to see how much they can remember.

Keep a record of the score to see who the winner is.

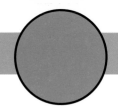

Language Summary

1. Meeting People

Lap 1

Hello, I'm Mike. What's your name?
Hello, Mike.
How old are you?
Where are you from?
Would you like to dance?

2. Agreeing/Disagreeing

I like it. So do I.
          Do you? I don't.
I haven't got any money. Neither have I.
                          Haven't you? I have.

3. Obligation/Necessity

You must do your homework.
You mustn't chew gum in class.
You need to wear comfortable shoes.
You needn't bring your camera. You can buy post cards.

4. Offering Help/Asking for Help

Could you carry this bag for me, please?
          Certainly!
          Sorry, I can't.
Shall I clean it for you? No, thanks, I can do it myself.
Can I give you a hand? Yes please.

5. Future Forms

They'll help you. Will he understand?
I'm going to study literature. Are you going to do it?

6. Instructions/Infinitive of Purpose

Colour one side of the strips of paper.
We use it to cut paper.

7. Present Perfect

Have you been to Chile? Yes, I have.
                         No, I haven't.

8. Giving Advice

You should save some money.
You shouldn't spend so much.
Why don't you ask your parents?
If I were you, I'd get a job.

9. Present Passives

What's it made of? It's made of gold.

1. Question Tags

Lap 2

You're French, aren't you?
He'll phone us, won't he?

2. Make/Let

They make us work hard.
They don't let us wear our favourite clothes.
He lets me wear my favourite clothes.
He doesn't make me get up early.

3. Comparatives and Superlatives

He was the smallest man in the world.
I've never seen a body as small as your husband's.
His son was smaller than him.
He wasn't as small as his sister.

4. First Conditional

If you move the camera, the snaps will come out blurred.

5. Suggestions

Let's go to the cinema. No, I've seen that film.
Why don't we go for a picnic?
We can go to Tommy's concert. That's a great idea!

6. Present Perfect Continuous

How long have you been saving?
I've been saving for six months.

7. Second Conditional

What would you do if you had a lot of money?
If I had a lot of money, I'd put it in the bank.

8. Past Passives

The telephone was invented by Graham Bell.

9. Relative Clauses

He's the boy I love.
He's the man who saved my life.

1

You are walking in the countryside. It is very warm, so you sit under a tree to rest. There is a cool breeze and you feel a little tired after the walk, so you fall asleep.

When you wake up, you are not in the countryside, you are in a forest!

You want to go home, so you get up and start walking.

Go to 15

2

You did not help the man. As you walk away, you feel bad. The poor old man looked very tired. You are very young. Of course you can help him! Go back and help him!

Go to 11

3

You walk around inside the house, knocking on every door but there is nobody there. Or is there? . . .

Go to 14

1

You are Mark O'Pole, an intrepid explorer. Ten days ago you tried to climb a mountain in Karabedor, an exotic country. Unfortunately you had an accident and all the people travelling with you died. The only thing you have managed to salvage is a compass. You have now got to the bottom of the mountain and now must decide which way to go.

a East, where you can see a jungle.
Go to 17

b South, where you can see a river.
Go to 23

c West, where you can see a desert.
Go to 10

2

This area is full of tigers and one of these has eaten you. You are dead now.

Go back to 19 and try again.

3

The water was very dirty and you couldn't see the crocodile that ate you in just five minutes.

Go back to 22 and try again

4

The bear approaches you and you are very frightened but you do not move.

Fortunately, this is a friendly bear and it licks your feet and lies down next to you. You pat it on the head and continue walking until you get to a lake.

Go to 21

5

You decided to knock on the door, but nobody answers.

What do you do?

a Try to get in.
Go to 16

b Continue walking in the forest.
Go to 13

6

When you attack the woman, she disappears. She was a witch! You are very frightened.

Go to 18

4

The old lady is very kind and she takes you to the nearest civilised town after giving you food and fresh water.

Go to 13

5

Unfortunately, the small private plane that was taking you to the nearest international airport crashed into a mountain.

Go back to 13 and try again

6

The members of the tribe living in the village are head hunters. They have killed you.

Go back to 17 and try again

7

You run very fast but the bear runs very fast too!

You soon get to a lake. What do you do?

a Jump into the lake.
Go to 21

b Climb up a tree.
Go to 17

8

You are afraid to move. A voice in your head tells you to run away but you cannot.

The woman catches you.

Go to 10

9

You decided to eat the cake. It is very nice. You are eating it when a strange woman appears.

What do you do?

a Attack her.
Go to 6

b Stand still and wait.
Go to 8

c Run away.
Go to 13

7

Walking along the river bank, you have got back to the desert where the river runs along a canyon.

Suddenly, there is an increase in the volume of water because it is raining heavily further west. You try to swim, but you are very weak and you drown.

**Go back to
15 and try again**

8

Walking through the jungle is very difficult because it is terribly hot and you have not got any water with you.

You are keeping alive by licking the dew on the tree leaves. You hope you can find your way to a civilized town soon.

Go to 24

9

You waited until it got dark to continue walking unnoticed by the natives. Unfortunately, the members of this tribe are head hunters and they hunt in the night.

They have caught you and you are now dead.

Go back to 17 and try again

10

She puts you in a cage, locks the door and walks away.

What do you do?

a Talk to her.
Go to 20

b Try to open the door.
Go to 12

11

You help the old man and he gives you a golden key.

The man tells you that it is the key to a castle and he takes you there.

Go to 22

12

You try to open the door but it is impossible. The cage is made of steel and the door is locked.

As you sit down to cry, you see the woman returning with some food for you.

Go to 20

Maze   Explorer

Lap 2

10

After hours walking through the desert, you have come to a small oasis. You think you are very lucky because you are very hot. Unfortunately, a hostile tribe of Bedouins are guarding the oasis. They are going to kill you.

Go back to 1 and try again

11

You thought you were very lucky to find a canoe by the river. Unfortunately, this canoe was abandoned because it was full of holes. After rowing for a few minutes, the canoe starts leaking and you are forced to swim back.

Go to 3

12

The smartly dressed man was a head hunter. He was wearing his last victim's clothes. He has killed you and now he is wearing your clothes.

Go back to 24 and try again

13

You continue walking in the forest. It is a very nice forest. There are many birds and it is not dark. You are enjoying your walk when, suddenly, in front of you, you see a bear.

What do you do?

a Run away.
Go to 7

b Stand still.
Go to 4

14

Suddenly you feel a strong hand on your shoulder. It is a strange woman. She looks like a witch!

You try to escape but you cannot. She is very strong!

Go to 10

15

As you walk, you see a pretty house. It looks like a cake, but it is a house. Maybe someone can help you find your way home.

What do you do?

a Knock on the door.
Go to 5

b Walk past the house.
Go to 13

13

The old lady has taken you to the town of San Lassaires. After a week recovering, you have to decide how to get to the nearest international airport.

You can:

a Go by boat.
Go to 16

b Go by plane.
Go to 5

c Go by car.
Go to 20

14

The native is a head hunter and when you approach him, he kills you.

Go to 24 and try again.

15

The bridge looked old and primitive, but you thought that it looked strong enough to walk over. You are now on the other side. What are you going to do?

a Walk East along the river bank.
Go to 21

b Walk West along the river bank.
Go to 7

c Continue walking South through the jungle.
Go to 8

16

You push the door and it opens easily.

Inside the house, there is a cake. It looks delicious. You are very hungry.

What do you do?

a Eat it.
Go to 9

b Leave it where it is.
Go to 3

c Put it in your pocket for later.
Go to 24

17

You are now sitting on a branch of the tree. The bear cannot climb up the tree, so after a few minutes, it goes away.

You climb down from the tree.
Go to 21

18

Suddenly, you feel a strong hand on your shoulder. It is the witch!

You try to escape but it is impossible.

Go to 10

16

You decided to go by boat to the nearest international airport. You are now at your local pub telling your friends about your adventures.

Write a letter to the kind lady you met in the jungle and thank her for saving your life.

17

You have been travelling for three days through the jungle in very difficult conditions. You need to get some food and some rest. There is a small village a few yards away from where you are. It is time for you to make another decision.

a Walk on and avoid the village.
Go to 19

b Wait until it gets dark and then continue walking.
Go to 9

c Go back to the village and ask for help.
Go back to 6

18

After a few days walking, you were very tired and you did not see that there was a tiger trap ahead of you.
You fell into the trap and after a couple of days you died because you did not have any water or food.

Go back to 19 and try again.

19

After swimming for half an hour you arrive at the other side of the lake. You are very tired, so you decide to lie down on the shore for a few minutes.

As you are resting, a very old man comes along. He is carrying a very heavy bag. He asks for help.

What do you do?

a Help him.
Go to 11

b Say that you are in a hurry and walk away.
Go to 2

20

You talk to the woman and she is very nice. She put you in the cage because she thought you were a thief. When you explain the situation to her, she lets you go.

Go to 13

21

You jump into the water and swim away from the shore. After half an hour, you come to a small island in the middle of a lake.

What do you do?

a Get on the island.
Go to 23

b Swim past the island.
Go to 19

19

You have decided to avoid the village. Now you have to decide again.

a Are you going to walk East?
Go to 18

b Are you going to go South?
Go to 22

c Are you going to go North?
Go to 2

20

Not long after you left the town your car broke down.

Go back to 13 and try again.

21

The scenery is very beautiful and the river is very noisy. You did not notice the waterfall ahead of you and you fall 300m to your death.

Go back to 15 and try again.

22

You open the door of the castle and, suddenly, you wake up. You are back in the countryside under a tree.

23

The island is very pretty. There are lots of flowers and birds there, but nothing else.

You rest for an hour and then continue swimming.
Go to 19

24

Now you've got food for later. What will you do next?

a Leave the house and continue walking in the forest.
Go to 13

b See if you can find someone in the house to ask them the way home.
To to 3

22

After a few days walking you have arrived at a river. What are you going to do now?

a Swim across.
Go to 3

b Use a canoe you can see abandoned by the river.
Go to 11

c Walk over a very old and very primitive bridge.
Go to 15

23

Swimming across the river was a mistake. The river was full of piranhas and a swarm of these little fish have eaten you in less than a minute.

Go back to 1 and try again.

24

Tired and thirsty you have arrived at a clearing in the jungle where there are three huts.
You need help and now you must decide which hut to go to.

a A hut covered in green leaves owned by a native wearing a loincloth.
Go to 14

b A hut made of mud owned by a very smartly dressed man.
Go to 12

c A hut made of wood owned by an old lady dressed like a witch.
Go to 4

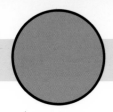

Pair work exercises

A Telephone Message   **Student A**

1 Phone your friend Mark to invite him to a party at your house on Saturday. You want to know if he can come or not.

2 Margaret is your sister. She is at the swimming baths now. Answer the phone and offer to take a message.

3 Phone Penny. You lent her your camera and now you'd like to have it back because you're going on an excursion.

4 Paul is your brother. He is having a bath. Answer the phone and offer to take a message.

Pair Work

Did you say 'right' or 'write'?   **Student A**

1 Student B has got the answers to these questions. Ask him/her to find them.
a Why did the window take an aspirin?
b Why did the schoolboy throw the clock out of the window?
c Why did the cook go to jail?
d Why aren't ghosts afraid?

2 Now student B will ask you some questions. Find the answers below.
1 Because the students were so bright. (bright/bright)
2 Because his tale was very sad. (tail/tale)
3 Because he wanted to save time.
4 Because he was very fast. (race/race)

Suggestions   Student A

1 Student B will suggest some activities. Read the information and respond accordingly.
– You love history.
– You don't like horror films.
– You don't like ants.
– You are terrified of insects.
– You never go on picnics.
– You're afraid of water.
– You can't play tennis.

2 Look at the pictures below and suggest things to do:

A Telephone Message   Student B

1 Mark is your brother. He is visiting a friend today. Answer the phone and offer to take a message.

2 Phone your friend Margaret to invite her to go to the cinema tomorrow. You've got tickets for 'Grammarman III'.

3 Penny is your sister. She is out shopping. Answer the phone and offer to take a message.

4 Phone your friend Paul to ask him to return the tape you lent him last week. You'd like to listen to it.

Tommy's trips   Student B

Here is a list of countries. Tommy has visited some of them. Work in pairs to complete the information on the list.

Remember: √ = yes   ✗ =no

Ask and answer questions like this:
A: Has he been to Thailand?
B: Yes, he has.
A: Has he been to Chile?
B: No, he hasn't.

Thailand	✓	Greece	✓
Chile	✗	Egypt	
Germany		China	
Turkey		America	✓
Japan	✗	Israel	✗
Colombia		Argentina	✗

An Interview   Student B

You are Chris Cross, a famous pop star

You have sung country music for two years but now you want to start singing rock and roll music. You want the reporter to mention this in the article.

You've got a boyfriend/girlfriend. He/she is a member of the Royal Family. Both of you want to keep your romance secret for now.

You have a very embarrassing habit: you suck your thumb when you are worried, when you watch T.V. or when you go to sleep. You don't want the reporter to find out about this habit.

You are going to give a charity concert at Wembley Arena. The money will go to the World Wildlife Fund. You love animals, especially wild animals like pandas or tigers. You think that people who wear furs are stupid. Make sure the reporter mentions this in the article.

When you've finished, write a letter to your boyfriend/girlfriend, telling him/her about the interview and about your plans for the future.

Did you say 'right' or 'write?' Student B

I Student **A** will ask you some questions. Choose the correct answer for each question from the list below.
1 Because he beat the eggs. (beat/beat)
2 Because it had a pane (pain/pane).
3 Because they don't believe in people.
4 Because he wanted to see time fly.

2 Now ask student **A** these questions. He/she has got the answers.
1 Why did the schoolboy put his watch in the piggy bank?
2 Why did the crocodile cry?
3 Why was Adam the first in the human race?
4 Why did the teacher wear sunglasses?

Pair Work

page 64

Two Famous People Student B

You have got some information about Tommy, but you need some information about Shamrock Holes. Ask student A for this information. When you finish, student A will ask you for some information.

Shamrock Holes
Ask questions like this:
How long has he been . . .?

investigating crime .... ?

living in Liverpool .... ?

collecting post cards .... ?

studying astronomy... ?

> Tommy has been singing with the Cats for two months. He moved to Southford with his parents when he was 1 year old. He started collecting sunglasses last year. He's been going to singing lessons for 5 years.

A Picture – A Story   Student B

You are going to read the description of a picture to student **A** and student **A** has to guess the story behind the picture. To find out the story, student **A** will ask you questions. You can only answer 'yes' or 'no'.

Here is your picture and story.

Read the description of the picture out to student **A**.
Picture: a woman is talking to a man and he is taking off his trousers.

Don't tell student A this story, but read it in silence.
Story: The woman is the man's wife. She's phoned him to tell him that their son has lost his pet snake and that the son can remember putting it in his father's trouser pocket.
Has student A guessed the story behind your picture?
Now you have to guess the story behind student A's picture.
Student A will describe a picture to you. You must find out the story behind that picture. To find out the story, you'll have to ask student A questions, but student A can only answer 'yes' or 'no.'